BLOCKS

BLOCKS

The Enlightened Way To Clear Writer's Block and Find Your Creative Flow

Tom Evans

First Published In Great Britain 2009
by Publishing Academy
www.publishingacademy.com

Permission to use the extract in Chapter 6
granted by Tony Buzan, the inventor of Mind Maps
(www.buzanworld.com)

To Louise for giving me copious amounts of time and space.

Contents

Praise

"This book offers some excellent strategies of overcoming writers' block. It's full of extremely useful and practical advice which will be of great benefit to any writer, both novice and professional. I was heartened to know that I already follow some of your advice. When I have a full days writing ahead of me, I always meditate for half an hour or so."

Steve Taylor, Author of Making Time,
www.stevenmtaylor.com

"Blocks is one of those books that not only works, but goes beyond what you expect. Not only will it stimulate your creativity and free you from writer's block but it will also inspire you to greater heights and motivate you into action as well. This treatise could well be a turning point for you! The audio visualisations are sublime and really consolidate the wisdom in the book."

Ron G Holland 'The Billion Dollar Biker',
Author of The Eureka Enigma, www.eureka-enigma.com

"You have really cracked this – it reads in a lovely chatty style, but in an informed and knowledgeable way, it absolutely works. It offers prospective writers a fabulous handbook to keep by them with real and relevant exercises and practices. Congratulations on a great book!"

Wendy Salter, Author of Herstoria and
Green Stones, www.wendysalter.com

"Blocks goes way beyond the subject of writer's blocks to overcome 'life blocks' of all kinds. You'll certainly become far more productive as an author with this book and you may just find you change your whole life while you're at it! I'm very proud to be publishing Tom's fantastic book."

Joe Gregory, Author, Publisher and Co-founder of The Publishing Academy, www.publishingacademy.com

"There is no other way to write a book. Tom injects a certain magic to the whole process. Tom has an amazing way of seeing the things that you don't see during the writing process, which helps unblock those writer's block moments. He leads you to dimensions that you had not even thought of yet. I now have restored belief in my writing ability and creativity."

Joanne Simpson, Author of They Thought It Was All Over, They Were Right

"Words can't explain how good Tom is at inspiring and helping a writer. Tom has made what I thought was impossible, possible and opened doors I thought could never open for me. He has unlocked my potential and I feel excited to be starting a new writing journey."

Sarah Lamb, Author of Appreciating Angels

"Tom has such a beautiful way with words."

Penny Power, Author of Know Me, Like Me, Follow Me, www.ecademy.com

"If you want to connect to, and unleash, your true creative potential, then Tom is your man. He's phenomenal."

Tina Bettison, Author of 100 Ways A Horse is Better Than A Man, www.tlbmedia.com

"Tom is a constant inspiration, source of ideas and realiser of your dreams - most notably the ones you don't know you have!"

Jackie Walker, The Divorce Coach,
www.thedivorcecoach.co.uk

"Tom is the 21st century prophet of clear guidance. His enthusiasm knows no bounds and his genuine authenticity is very refreshing."

Colin Richards, Inventor of The Game of 33,
www.gameof33.com

"In my opinion, Tom is one of the top three people in the world to have a 1-2-1 with."

Thomas Power, Chairman of Ecademy,
www.ecademy.com

"The power of Tom's book to unleash creativity is brilliant and his explanation of the power of Mind Mapping on page 39 is particularly apropos as it has bugged me for ages why Mind Maps work. Well done!"

Bill Liao, Author of Stone Soup, www.neo.org

Acknowledgements

Like many books, this is not a solo effort. I am not referring here to any external guidance from the superconsciousness and future versions of me. That said, I do give loads of thanks in that particular direction too and to all the *future me's* who have played a part.

This book came about with help from many wonderful people in the present, and near past, who I have met on my path to becoming and being an author and I am grateful to them all. My thanks goes to:

Jenny Littlejohn, Lisa Turner, Jackie Walker and Wendy Salter for your guidance.

Lynn Clay for the excellent exercise on what foods to eat for inspiration.

Tony Buzan, Steve Taylor and Bill Liao for the superb and influential quotes that changed my mind.

My soul sister, Jo Simpson, for helping me hone my new skills and talents.

Thomas Power for the idea for the title and Penny Power for connecting so many good hearts and minds through Ecademy.

Vanessa Warwick, Nick Tadd, David Stevens, Steve Nobel, Damien Senn, Joanna Penn and Julia McCutchen for all the thought provoking interviews.

My publishers, Debbie Jenkins and Joe Gregory, for making easy what some over-complicate

Sylvia Howe for your editing eye and perspicacity.

The Kryon School in Germany for permission to use the crystal symbols in the book.

The collective wisdom which manifests as Wikipedia in helping to compile the glossary.

Wellington and Reuben for insisting on taking me on regular walks – extra dog biscuits coming your way.

Preamble

*"The role of a writer is not to
say what we all can say, but
what we are unable to say."*

Anais Nin

Words are wonderful.

No matter which language you speak, the marks you make with a pen on paper, or with a typewriter or computer, are a representation of your thoughts.

Some time later, perhaps centuries, someone else can read them and act upon them. Perhaps they will laugh or cry or be entertained, educated or enlightened.

We take this form of thought transmission for granted.

The internal dialogue in your head, which is externally silent, gets replayed inside someone else's head miles away or years apart in time. It could even be described as a form of telepathy.

What we also take for granted is that it is words themselves that give us the ability to be self-aware and to think. You will see later in this book that this very same process can also block our ability to write.

Now, for a writer, one of the best ever feelings is when the words you have written inspire someone to write their own words, perhaps even in the form of a review of your book or a comment on your blog. Your writing may even inspire them to write a book of their own.

Elements of this book, for example, were inspired by at least 10 others which results in the propagation of their thoughts.

I have heard it said: "The only thing you take with you is your evolution and the only thing you leave behind is your art."

Imagine how a long departed writer like Dickens or Shakespeare would feel if they knew their words were still inspiring new generations of writers. When they wrote their words they had no idea that people would be repeating their lines on television and film.

Now when it comes to writing, there are four classifications of people in the world.

There are people who have both written and published. This group includes, of course, literary giants as well as many a celebrity author.

It's a fair bet that they are far outnumbered by those who have written something and not had it published. The numbers of books that have been started and not finished far exceed the billions of books that have actually seen the light of day.

There are even people who have published but not written – they are called publishers.

What is incalculable are the numbers of people since the emergence of cuneiform script, or even earlier, who have neither written nor published anything.

In this modern, wired world the old excuse for not writing because of the fear of the dreaded publisher's rejection letter, or apathy, has vanished.

Blocks

With print on demand technology, and the ability to self-publish via blogs and ebooks, to become a published author you just need to make the decision you want to write.

Naturally you also have to decide what you are going to write and when you are going to write.

No matter which of these classifications you fall into, at some point you may come across the bane of every scribe - the dreaded writer's block.

For some, a distraction like going for a walk is enough to get them back on track. Others can't loosen those mental cogs whatever they do, and this book is for them.

There is nothing like a deadline to block creative flow. So the thoughts, musings and exercises in this book are aimed at experienced and published writers as well as those starting out on their literary path.

The techniques you will learn apply to any style of writing or creative process. If you are writing a sales proposal, a blog or even an advert to sell something on eBay, there is some help here. If you are an artist, a musician, a script writer or a student writing an essay, this book is for you too.

As you will see, my approach to clearing writer's block is to introduce a new and holistic way of thinking and being, and to show an alternative way to look what a block represents.

You have heard it said, I am sure, that we only use five per cent of our brain, or even less. If this is true, what is the rest of our brain for, and how do we tap into it?

The simple exercises in this book will show you how you can begin to expand not only your mind but also your horizons.

You will not only learn how to manage your time to help you write but how to stretch it so that you write in one hour what for many would take a day.

You will learn the techniques of Whole Brain Thinking and how to get the left and right hemispheres working in synchronistic harmony.

You will see and experience how this leads to altered states of consciousness where you enter a mode where you are in the flow I call Whole Mind Not-thinking.

You will read about the latest (and ancient) theories about where our thoughts come from, and how you can tap into those famous light bulb moments on demand.

You will learn how da Vinci, Newton and Einstein experienced prescience – and why the word should be perhaps hyphenated to pre-science.

It should be noted too that a form of writer's block continues *after* a book is written and published. A writer must be their book's ambassador and publicist so it gets read by lots of people.

This book has been written to help authors undergo personal transition, enlightenment and evolution by writing their book. If their book subsequently enlightens, educates and entertains readers, then that is a real bonus.

My overall approach is that, to make this happen, blocks are to be welcomed and embraced so that we learn from them and evolve.

This book is based on over three years' experience of working with writers in various states of blockage on a one-to-one basis and in my *Unleash the Book Inside* workshops.

It is also, of course, based on my own experience as a blocked writer and author.

I've been there, done that, got the T-Shirt. Even when writing this book, I had to face a few old familiar demons.

This book is an exploration and represents a work in progress.

I encourage feedback and reviews (negative or positive) from readers, and especially writers. Only by learning what works, and what doesn't can I extend and improve as a writer and a mentor.

The exercises in this book are designed to free up your creativity and to introduce you to a new way of thinking, being and doing.

As nature has proven for billennia, there is no better way to evolve but by trial, error, iteration and reinvention.

Tom Evans
www.thebookwright.com
Surrey Hills, UK, 2009

Tom Evans

How To Read This Book

There are many different ways to approach this book. You can choose the one that suits you best.

Like all books, you can read it sequentially, breaking off at each chapter to do the simple exercises that each contains.

You could savour the book, taking in one chapter a day so that in your sleep and dreams the learnings instill themselves into your unconscious mind and cellular neurology.

There is even a chapter on using dreams as part of the writing process that will help you create while you sleep.

Or you can read the theory and explanation in one or two sessions and come back and do the exercises later.

You may even find that reading just one chapter, even the first one, is enough to set you up and catapult you into that written and published category. You can also dive straight into a chapter that interests you, wherever it is in the book.

Why not be radical?

This book is designed so it can be read forwards or backwards, so you can start with the last chapter and end up here.

You will find resources on my web site such as links to software tools and Mind Map templates for the exercises. There are companion audio visualisations to help you enter altered and heightened states of mind.

That said, no special technology or extraordinary expense is required. A journal or reporter's note pad to complete the exercises in the book is useful, however.

As a reader aid, we have emboldened words that might be unfamiliar to you and you will find explanations for them in a glossary at the end of the book.

Chapter 1

So Why Write A Book?

"If we wait for the moment when everything is ready, we shall never begin."

Ivan Turgenev

One of the main ways to avoid writer's block is not to write a book at all. If you don't try, you can't possibly get stuck.

This is probably what keeps most people in the not-written and not-published category.

My guess is that the fact you are reading this at all means that this doesn't apply to you.

If you are going to all the effort of writing a book, I think you'll agree it would be a good idea to write 'a great book'. This thought alone will help you to maintain a high level of motivation throughout the writing process, and beyond.

The best way to deal with writer's block is not to get stuck in the first place.

Many people want to write a book to make money. This aim, though perfectly laudable, can be enough to create a blockage.

I believe there is a healthier and more productive approach to making your book a success.

An alternative approach is to aim for the two main benefits to be gained from writing a book as being the personal transformation you achieve as a writer and the enlightenment and entertainment you impart to the reader.

When you succeed in delivering both of these, the financial reward you seek will come.

And not just from book sales.

From a purely personal perspective, researching or dreaming up your book is a journey that is rewarding in its own right.

The sense of pride when each milestone is reached is simply amazing.

As you go from first draft to edited manuscript, through proof reading and typesetting and on to publication, you will grow in stature and sense of purpose.

As a published author, your friends and family, work colleagues, partners and clients see you in a new light. You become a domain expert in the eyes of the press, TV and radio.

New doors will open for you as your book connects with people who you simply wouldn't otherwise have met.

Your book becomes the best business card you have ever had and you will be surprised how it brings in revenue from unexpected sources. This is true for fiction and non-fiction books.

When you receive your first reviews and realise how your words affect other people, people who aren't your friends and family, you cannot help but beam with pride.

One such review of my first book made me feel I had really arrived as an author. One man said:

"Stunning. I cried. That's all."

I was hooked and these words, and words like them, inspired me to write even more.

Exercise 1: Your Guiding Motivation

How do you go about writing a great book?

How do you write a book that people tell other people to read?

First you need to look inside yourself and examine why you are writing a book in the first place.

Any publisher you pitch to will want to know the answers to these questions anyway so it's worth considering them even if you are self publishing or writing an e-book.

What you and any potential publisher will want to know is this:

- Why you?
- Why now?
- What's different about your book?
- What genre does it fit into?
- What other books is it like?
- What books do you like?

- What are your influences?

- Who is your target reader?

- What will the reader learn and take away with them?

- What ideas do you have to find your target readers?

- What do you plan to do under your own initiative to promote and sell the book?

- What are your aspirations as an author?

- What would you like to happen as a result of writing your book?
  - For you
  - For your business
  - For your readers
  - For the planet

What Should You Write?

Armed with the answers to these questions, you should now spend time considering exactly what you should be writing.

For example, you might want to write a personal development book to support your business or sell at your workshops. The natural format for this would be a self-help manual with explanations of your theories and perhaps some case studies and exercises.

It is worth considering if your message could be conveyed more powerfully in an allegorical or metaphorical story. Examples such as *Who Moved My Cheese* by Spencer Johnson and *The Way of the*

Wizard by Deepak Chopra are a testament to the power of this lateral approach.

Story telling is a natural and fun way to approach writing and gives you much creative freedom. Books using such an allegorical approach pack quite a punch, however short they are.

Conversely, if you are planning to write a work of fiction, could it be easier to reach your potential readers with a more factual approach?

Much consideration should be given to the length of your book.

Will 200,000 words of eloquent prose be a turn off for your reader?

For example, I managed to write a whole life story in just 33 stanzas of four lines each that can be read in just 15 minutes, perhaps while commuting. It is amazing how the reader will fill in the gaps.

If you are writing non-fiction, consider what ancillary information you need to impart and the best way to convey it? Perhaps case studies and exercises will be useful here.

Do you want to take the reader on a journey? Your book could be time-based. For example, it could be entitled, *A year in the life ...* or *Change your world in seven days ...*

Initially, I specifically wrote this book with 14 chapters so it can easily be re-entitled, *Get Rid of Writer's Block in Two Weeks ... or less.* That was my plan at least but another chapter crept in as it is often prone to do.

You can test the market for titles like these by blogging or e-publishing your book.

Another natural structure may work for you or you might just like things with a certain number of components, parts and chapters.

You should also think about books like yours that have already been published. It's important to tread a fine line between plagiarism and advancement of art and knowledge.

I read a lot in the field I write in and always strive to add a new dimension to other works or to introduce them in a new context. If you do want to lift material, there are conventions and legalities to be addressed and adhered to.

You can also copy and emulate literary styles you like but using entirely your own words, ideas and plot lines. I love the way Paulo Coelho, Kurt Vonnegut and Douglas Adams write and my prose style aims to be a synthesis and homily to their great art.

I hope this chapter has given you some inkling about what you might write. Now it's time to move on to look at how you make the time to write it

CHAPTER 2

Making Time To Write

"Much may be done in those little shreds and patches of time which every day produces, and which most throw away."

Charles Caleb Colton

By the end of this book, you will have learnt techniques to expand time so you achieve amazing feats of creativity by writing *in the zone*.

In my experience, writers who are poor at managing their time to write also struggle with time management in general.

Before we tackle the fundamental changes in mindset you need for this to happen, it is worth looking at the basics of time management.

There are many excellent books on this subject and I have listed some in the recommended reading at the back of this book. If time management is an issue for you, then ironically you may not find the time to read a book on the subject. So, to save you time, I've summarised the tips that are most salient to writers in this purposely short chapter.

As for all the techniques discussed in this book, there are great life benefits to be gained by tackling this at the start of a new writing project.

By doing so, you end up with a real win-win situation.

Exercise 2: Time Management

First, make three lists.

1. What habits do you want to break in your life?

2. What external circumstances and factors are stopping you from getting the time to write your book?

3. For the next working day or week, write down what you do in half hourly intervals.

Writing this list can be enough to inspire you to take action. You may find you are spending time on computer games or that you should really be delegating at work or at home.

Let's say your book is a similar size to this one of 14 chapters or so. Now bear in mind that I have done years of research and know what I want to write about. Similarly, if your book is non-fiction it is likely to be written around what you know. If it's fiction, you are either basing it on life experiences or making it up, writing it from the heart.

Irrespective of your writing style, a typical chapter of a book runs for between 1200 to 2400 words or four to eight pages of a typical paperback book. This rule is far from hard and fast though.

Blocks

Once you are in the zone and you either know or have researched your material, then you can write such a chapter in anything between two hours, or a half a day. Note, to do this, it's advisable to resist the temptation to edit as you go along.

This means that a book with say 14 chapters will take you no more than seven days of time to write. You can, of course, treat yourself to a writing break and take a much needed holiday. This is a real win-win.

So let's say you allocate half a day a week to write your book, a book of this size will take you no more than three to four months to write. You can, of course, do what I did for this book and write the first draft in two weeks. I will leave it to reader feedback to see if I have been effective in my aims.

The other essential time management trick is to be focused and disciplined. It is said that each time you flip from one task to another, it takes up an additional five minutes on top of the tasks themselves.

I think it is worse than this for a writer as you can take even more time to get back in your groove and to remember where you were going with your stream of thought.

The first thing to establish is when you are at your most creative in the day and when you are least likely to be interrupted.

For me, the morning works doubly well as I use my dream time and a morning dog walk as part of my writing process. You will learn techniques to use your dream time and how to meditate while walking (or exercising) later on in this book.

You should establish how you would like to write your book. Some people prefer pen and paper or, if you are like me and can't read your own writing, use a computer. Others prefer to dictate their books. The technology to do this is either free, or inexpensive, and has the added bonus of producing an audio version of the book, or a podcast, at the same time.

Whichever route you take, make sure your phones are switched off or on answer phone before you start.

Switch off your email.

Ask your friends, family and colleagues to respect your writing time. You may even get offers from people who would like to proof read or edit your work.

When you do start and finish writing, pat yourself on the back for what you have done. You deserve it. Unlike so many people, you have taken yourself one step nearer to publication.

Runners tackle a marathon psychologically by taking one step at a time and covering one mile at a time. At the halfway point, they say to themselves that they just need to do the same again. At 19 or so miles in, they think they just have a quarter marathon to complete – a mere training run.

Writing is a similar discipline. One word at a time is all it takes and it should be remembered that less is sometimes more, which is a good point for me to move on to the next chapter.

Chapter 3

Getting In The Groove

"The more I practice, the luckier I get."

Golfer Gary Player

The more you write, the better you get at it. Not only that, you will find your vocabulary improves. If you choose not to practice, the opposite can happen.

Like all mental activity, writing uses specific areas in the brain.

Simply doing it brings blood with oxygen and nutrients to the relevant part of the brain which exercises, strengthens and multiplies connections between neurons.

If you want to run that marathon, you start with shorter runs to build up stamina, muscle strength and endurance. You may also get tips from people who have done it.

Unlike marathon running, you can stop for a rest at any time when writing and begin again when the mood takes you.

This next exercise is to be repeated daily and is designed to work the bits of your brain that may be neglected. It's a technique recommended by Julia Cameron in her book The Artist's Way which I shamelessly borrow from and blatantly plug here.

The book has loads of other great tips and I highly recommend it.

Julia recommends you write something every day, ideally just after waking and in a quiet environment. She calls them "morning pages".

If you want to make them your midday or evening pages, that's fine and feel free to write more than once a day. If you wake in the early hours, writing can be cathartic and help you get back to sleep once you've downloaded those inner thoughts.

You may also find that writing a blog each day works for you. As mentioned before, many books have emerged from blogging.

What happens is that all of a sudden you see that a collection of your writings and musings can be collated into a whole book and, without knowing it, you've written it. This may be a selection of short stories or poems. It may be a self-help or personal development book like this one which came from a set of PowerPoint exercises I run in my workshops that I then scripted and narrated for an online course.

Breaking the writing of a book down like this also allows you to serialise it, either in a magazine or perhaps in an email autoresponder sequence.

Exercise 3: Getting In The Groove

Complete two to three sheets in an A5 reporter's pad or a couple of sheets of A4 every morning. You can write anything you like; here are some examples:

- Base your writing on your dreams

- Describe the events of yesterday, especially what was good

- Describe your ideal day or be creative & make up your best day ever

- Describe the room you are in – or the room you would like to be in

- Have a go at the next chapter of a book you are stuck on

- Write some poetry

- Write a blog post

- Write an entertaining or erudite Tweet each day on *www.twitter.com* or why not Tweet a whole story as I did

- Write a story in just Six Words or Six Sentences and submit it to these two sites
  - o *www.sixwordstories.net*
  - o *www.sixsentences.blogspot.com*

Spend between 10 & 20 minutes on this exercise – or, if you find you get in flow, keep writing. You will be amazed what comes from this process.

Active Reading

Another crucial skill for writers is to read, and to read regularly.

Reading as a writer requires a different mindset to reading as someone who does not write.

This doesn't mean you have to read everything with a critical eye, like a literary critic, or to take twice as long over it. You just have to become aware of your feelings and thoughts when reading something. Specifically, pay attention to something you enjoyed or found interesting.

When you find a book you really like, take time to re-read sections of it. Pay attention to several things that you may have been only unconsciously aware of:

- The cover of the book
- The font type and size
- The way the text is laid out on the page
- The language used
- Read the opening paragraph of the introduction or a section you particularly liked again

With these in mind, describe your feelings:

- What do you think about the book?
- How does this make you think and feel about the author?
- What do you feel in your gut?

- What do you sense in your heart?

- What is going on in your head?

- What new ideas does thinking like this bring to you?

If it helps, write these down in your journal and repeat this exercise, at least mentally, every time you read something that inspires you.

You can try it out on this book. If you feel like it, try the same exercise on something you *didn't* like. Pay particular attention to the points in a book where you get lost or bored.

You will see later on how you can use this exercise so that your writing instils specific feelings and thoughts in the reader.

Tom Evans

CHAPTER 4

So What's Stopping You?

"Publishing your work is important.
Even if you are giving a piece to some
smaller publication for free, you will
learn something about your writing.
The editor will say something. Friends
will mention it. You will learn."

Tim Cahill

The exercises in the previous chapters are snapshots of the work we do in my workshops. They are normally enough to get authors off and writing. If that's happened to you and you don't even read the rest of this book, I will have achieved my aim.

That said, I know when people get back to their daily lives, things seem to get in the way of writing their book.

How do I know this? Because I've been there. I have been brilliant at inventing more important things to do than write.

Perhaps your room is a mess? OK, then tidy it, and then get down to writing.

Do you need to go to the supermarket, make lunch or write a letter? Then do it, but not in the time you have set aside for writing.

You can so easily become a busy fool or, if you are like me, put the needs of others (and your bank account) ahead of getting on with the writing of your books. There is nothing wrong with this, it's a fact of life, especially in these credit crunchy days.

Make no mistake, writing your book does not guarantee you instant riches and retirement. Like the lottery, you have to play to win.

But by writing and publishing something, however small, you will learn your craft and about the vagaries of the publishing industry.

The literary world is full of authors who only made it through tenacity and persistence. Some also only achieve fame posthumously. While this might not be entirely comforting, think of how you can leave a cultural legacy for the world and perhaps a financial legacy for your family.

Speaking personally, I cashed all my pensions in early before they lost even more money and I plan not only to make my writings my passive income but also to have a life style that supports what is essentially a hobby.

Apart from financial considerations, you may have a full time job or a family to look after.

You may have both.

I am a great believer in the win-win situation as a motivator.

Forgetting for a moment about the benefit of having a book published, this next exercise is designed to find out what will stop you from getting your book written.

In the second part of the exercise you will see the collateral benefits writing your book will give you in other areas in your life.

Exercise 4: Identifying Blocks

List the things that are currently preventing you from getting started with a book. Here are some examples:

- Full time job
- Family commitments
- Untidy office
- No computer at home
- Needing to do some research first
- Confidence in writing
- Lack of self esteem
- Fear of the unknown, ridicule, failure or success

Now list things in your life you would like to change, perhaps some bad habits:

- Not getting enough exercise
- Watching too much television
- Issues at work
- Family or relationship problems
- Playing computer games

Finally, write down how you would feel if you managed to not only write and publish a book but also deal with these issues in your life.

At the end of this book, we will bring these themes to a conclusion and you will see how reading this book and writing yours was such a pivotal point in your life.

It may well be that by reading the next chapters and completing the exercises, you find the change you were seeking starts to happen.

We are looking at new concepts about how your mind works and where ideas and thoughts come from. You will also see that both being creative and being blocked are patterns, or **gestalts**, that become fixed in our neurology.

Being in one state or the other is simply a choice and involves just a flip in our thinking.

CHAPTER 5

Whole Brain Thinking

"Each hemisphere is indeed a conscious system in its own right, perceiving, thinking, remembering, reasoning, willing, and emoting, all at a characteristically human level. Both the left and the right hemisphere may be conscious simultaneously in different, even in mutually conflicting, mental experiences that run along in parallel."

Roger Wolcott Sperry

Have you have ever watched a Tom & Jerry cartoon and seen a devil appearing on one shoulder and an angel on the other? You may not have noticed but it is common urban mythology for the devil to be on the left and the angel on the right.

For a writer, the devil might whisper things like, "You don't have time to write a book" and "Who would want to read anything you write anyway?"

At the same time, the angel is giving you ideas and inspirations and encouragement. You are stuck somewhere in the middle of this tug of war and, as result, might not get anything done.

If this sounds like you, don't fret. It's a byproduct of our evolution and is designed to protect us and keep us alive. Fortunately, as you will see in the exercises in this chapter and the next, it is relatively simple to overcome.

In the 60s and 70s, a Nobel Prize winning neurobiologist called Professor Roger Sperry discovered that different functions seem to reside on different sides of the brain. It has now seeped into popular psychology that there are left-brained people and right-brained people.

You may also see a trend for this to be mirrored in masculine and feminine behaviour. For example, on BBC News at least, the male newsreader always sits on the left of the female anchor.

This by the way doesn't mean all men are logical and women are creative - each of us has a differing mix of masculine and feminine. It is more observable as ego-led or ego-bound behaviour and heart-felt or gut-led activity. This is something that we will explore later when we discover how to tap into our **vestigial minds**.

The left brain is logical and controlling - the hemisphere of reason. The right hemisphere is creative and intuitive. You might think that the left brain would be the one to stop you writing a book, which is why the devil speaks in the left ear.

Well, you could also argue the logical left could say, "Write a book, it will make us rich."

Conversely the right hemisphere could be equally creative about writing your book or inventing excuses and diversions why you shouldn't. It's perhaps of interest that I was particularly creative about doing everything I could think of to avoid writing this particular chapter.

In passing, just notice that it feels OK to use the word "us" when referring to internal dialogues like this.

As it transpires, what is grandly named **hemispheric lateralisation of brain function** is a gross simplification yet it remains a handy model from which to begin banishing writer's block forever.

In later chapters, we will cover a model not just for he brain but for the mind, which is even more powerful in the context of tapping into unlimited creativity and inspiration.

Sperry and others did detailed research into a structure called the **corpus callosum** which connects the left and right hemispheres. It is common practice to start brain research with the treatment of the mentally ill, and they found they could treat epileptics with intractable *grand mal* seizures by surgically severing the corpus callosum.

There are rumours that Einstein's brain, which was embalmed, had a particularly large number of connections across the two hemispheres. Stories about Einstein's brain have seeped into mythology, so this needs to be taken with a pinch of salt, but it might be true.

What is generally agreed is that we only use portions of our brain at particular times. Some say we use less than five per cent or even as little as one per cent. This is bandied around as a criticism when it is more likely an evolutionary power-saving mechanism and self-protection strategy. Nature is a master at efficiency so why expend more energy than necessary.

What is known is that we automate repetitive actions like driving, and even using a keyboard as I am now, by forming neural pathways. At a lower level in the brain, functions such as breathing and keeping our heart beating have brain circuitry dedicated to this task.

The patterns we store help to keep us alive and protect us. This is shared between brain function in the lower reptilian stem and our evolved higher cortex. This is why, when we need precious blood supply, we might faint so that precious blood supply is rooted to the lower brain.

In the context of writer's block, if you were ever criticised at school for writing a bad essay or being late in submitting one, a wonderful self-protection strategy is not to write one at all. What is happening here is that neural pathways are set up which reinforce behaviour to keep us alive.

Sometimes though, short-term survival strategies don't necessarily serve our long-term needs.

The way around this block in writing is simple - start writing again. Publish blogs, short stories and articles. You may find that, instead of criticism, you get praise. If by some chance you do get shot down in flames, I will show you strategies later on to deal with this; one powerful one is to re-engage with your vestigial minds.

In preparation for the creative writing exercises later in the book, it's a fair assumption that no matter what model of the brain is true, we are better off using as much of our brain as possible. It's also a good bet that if different areas of the brain do indeed conflict with each other, and reason and logic can suppress creativity, **whole brain thinking** is a good thing to do.

In the next chapter, you will discover how **Mind Mapping** is the best possible tool when it comes to encouraging whole brain thinking. In preparation for this, it's time to get physical.

Exercise 5: Walking & Cross Crawling

Each neuron in our brain needs a blood supply to bring it nutrients. Otherwise, it will either die or, at the very least, become dormant and atrophy. This can happen as we age.

A simple and effective way to keep our brain active is to exercise. This doesn't mean a strenuous workout at a gym.

Just walking for 20 to 30 minutes a day is enough and, if you can, at a pace that gets you just short of being breathless.

Walking not only increases heart rate but blood flows to parts of your body and brain that it doesn't normally reach. I often go for a walk with clients and it is amazing how a good walk frees up the most stubborn blocks.

What walking also does is move the **cerebrospinal fluid** around so that our brains float and quite literally take the weight off our minds.

A specific type of walking seems to move it around even more, and increases the connections and communication between right and left hemispheres.

This exercise is in two parts which can be done separately, or combined if you feel particularly energetic. It seems appropriate linguistically to call them steps.

Step 1: Walking

If you are able, go for a 20 to 30 minute walk each day, ideally before you start to write or in between gaps in writing.

For at least five minutes of the walk, swing your arms from side to side in front of your body. Depending on where you are or your physical ability, this movement can be as small or large as you feel comfortable with.

Step 2: Cross Crawling

You can do this exercise in the comfort of your own home and it important that you do it slowly.

1. Stand with your arms to the side and let the tension fall from your body. Feel the floor with your feet.

2. Now bend your right leg at the knee and swing your left arm in front of you across your navel

and touch your left elbow to your right knee. Or as close as you can manage at this stage.

3. Let your right leg fall gently and your left arm return and now bend your left leg at the knee and touch your right elbow to the left knee. Again make sure your left arm crosses your navel.

4. Try to repeat the exercise 15 to 20 times for each side.

If you find it difficult or you seem to get your sides mixed up like tapping your head and rubbing your stomach, don't worry. This just means your left and right hemispheres really need this exercise. Either really slow the movements down or try it lying down. It will come in time.

I first did this exercise over 10 years ago and after the exercise I briefly started mirror writing. This is often a trait seen in those categorised with dyslexia. If it happens to you, take it as a sign that new pathways are opening up in your brain. Incidentally, the exercises in the next chapter are perfect for those who feel any dyslexic tendencies are blocking them from writing.

Note if you are physically infirm or unwell and either of these exercises is either impossible or likely to cause you harm, consult with your doctor or medical advisor before undertaking them.

If you cannot do either exercise, you can actually get some benefit by closing your eyes and imagining you are carrying them out.

Such is the power of the mind, as you will see later.

Tom Evans

CHAPTER 6

Mapping Your Mind

"It is my firm belief that every brain is, by nature, a Mind Mapper! The fact that a baby learns a language is evidence confirming that it must learn by multi-sensual images and their radiating associations. I also believe that everyone contains the full set of multiple intelligences."

Tony Buzan

Mind Maps are useful and elegantly simple devices.

Although there are many good software-based Mind Mapping tools on the market, some of the best Mind Maps are done with just pen and paper.

The reason for this is that some people can end up in a left brained mode simply by engaging with a computer keyboard, screen and mouse. When we have a pen or pencil in our hands not only do we use different neural pathways in our brains but the map manifests into physical, as opposed to virtual, reality. This leads to a better chance of your book being finished and published. On this note, if you do use computer software, print your maps out and stick them on a notice board or wall.

When it comes to whole brain thinking, their impact is explosive in the context of the creativity they seem to unleash. They are also really useful for aiding memory and brilliant for anyone studying and revising. If you do have children, my advice is to get them Mind Mapping as soon as possible.

In essence, Mind Maps are simple drawings or sketches of associations you hold between things in your mind. They normally start with a central topic, either in words or even better if expressed as an image. You then draw branches off from that image of the concepts that spawn from the central image.

So if you Mind Mapped something relatively trivial like a shopping list you might have a central image of a shopping trolley and branches such as fruit & veg, household, frozen food, beer & wine, dairy and desserts.

You can see what my typical shopping list is like. To make it even more memorable, you can use images of products on each branch.

What makes such a trivial Mind Map so powerful is that with a little training, you can forget to take the shopping list along, yet easily memorise all of its contents. I always Mind Map any talk I give on a single sheet of paper and am then able to reproduce all the points I want to get across without any notes or slides.

Where Mind Maps really come into their own is in the area of creativity and especially free-flow brainstorming where previously hidden associations appear like magic.

The left brain is your navigator through life and says to the right brain, "Aha, a map! I like maps, leave this to me, I'll handle it."

While the left brain is thus kept busy, the right brain seizes the opportunity to sneak under the left's radar to unleash its full creativity.

Of course, this is a gross over-simplification as you will see later. The whole left and right brain model is somewhat limited and there is a much more useful model of the brain, and mind, to use in the context of creativity. That said, thinking even in this simplistic kind of way about our own ability to think seems to have a beneficial effect in itself. Our brains have an ability to form new neural pathways in an instant. This is a phenomenon known as **brain plasticity**. This happens when we learn a new skill and commit it to unconscious memory and is very beneficial for victims of strokes, for example. What is perhaps even more remarkable is that just thinking about our own consciousness in a new way seems to encourage this rewiring to take place. This is a bit like changing a tyre on your car whilst driving on a motorway.

Mind Maps stimulate this process; a single word or image on the map is enough to fire off new associations that were perhaps previously suppressed or idle.

Our brain is fantastic at recognising patterns and especially images, which is how we can sometimes remember a face but not a name.

As an example, the following map contains all the points made in this book.

MINDMAPS

NEUROLOGY

EMBEDDING THOUGHTS

QUANTUM

COLLAPSE

PAST

FUTURE

ENTANGLEMENT

VISUALISATIONS

DESTINY

PURPOSE

AKASKIC

DESTINY

PURPOSE

FEAR-LESS

THROAT

HEART

RE-MINDING

GUT

SIMPLE

CUMULATIVE

RE-USEABLE

EXERCISES

Blc

FUN

BREATHI

FOOD

EDUTAINING

WATER

EXERCISE

EXPANSIVE

WALKING

CROSSCRAWLIN

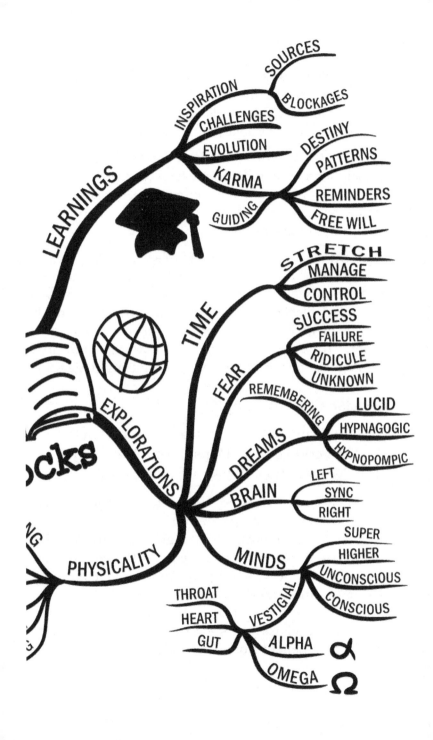

A Mind Map awakens dormant neural pathways and forges new ones at the same time. For this reason, it's advisable to use single words or single images per branch as this gives more flexibility in onward associations.

Note that, for the visually impaired and others, associations of sounds or smells have the same effect as images. Also for some known as **synaesthetes**, the senses can get muddled; numbers can appear as colours, or tastes as sounds.

This shows that the brain is plastic in the way it creates associations and we can use this to help us with writer's block. By the end of this book, you will learn that blocks themselves are good for you, really helpful in making you a better and more expressive writer. To take the next step towards this new paradigm in our thinking, let's do some Mind Mapping.

Exercise 6: Mind Mapping

> **To augment this exercise you can listen to 'Embedding Mind Maps in Your Neurology' MP3 Visualisation. Details at the back of the book.**

If you are new to Mind Mapping, I advise you do these exercises on paper and pen. If you are experienced and have Mind Mapping software, feel free to use it but with one caveat. As I mentioned, for some people, just sitting in front of a computer, keyboard and mouse throws them into left-brain mode. Unless you use a computer completely intuitively, I advise you stick to hand drawn maps to get the best benefit from the exercise.

To get the hang of Mind Maps, I'd like you to do two maps, one on a subject you know where you will have free rein, and one on a subject you are potentially still exploring. For this latter map, you will base your map on a suggested structure. The reason for this is that it's really useful to experience the two slightly different states of thinking which ensue from each approach.

So in preparation, ideally get some A3 paper and some coloured paper and pens.

Map 1: Draw an image in the middle of the paper that represents you (which could be a photograph you stick on the paper). Now map your life so far and note that I am being specific about not giving any more instruction than that.

Map 2: Go back to the exercise you did in Chapter 1, and add the answers that apply to a map like the one on the next page. Feel free to make as many sub-branches as you wish and you can even take the branch, "What will your reader learn?" and make that into a whole new map.

Take time over both these exercises and when you have finished the second map, you may like to listen to *Embedding Mind Maps in Your Neurology* in the MP3 Visualisation Pack.

Incidentally, another way to get the left and right hemispheres in sync is to use what is known as brain entrainment music. This works by presenting slightly out of phase audio signals into each ear and I use it as the background for all my audio visualisations.

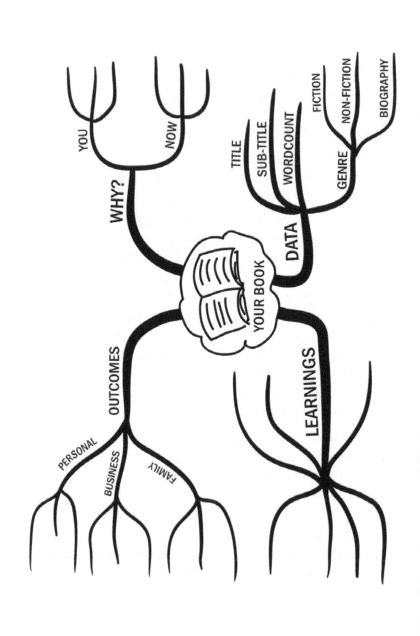

CHAPTER 7

Whole Mind Not-Thinking

"Meditation is the dissolution of thoughts into eternal awareness or pure consciousness without objectification, knowing without thinking, merging finitude in infinity."

Voltaire

We use maps and models every day to make sense of our complex world. For example, imagine you landed at Narita Airport outside Tokyo and I told you the cheapest place to buy electronic gadgets is a place called Akiabara. Armed with this information, the metro map, and a credit card but without being able to speak Japanese, you would be able to both find Akiabara and a bargain.

The model of the brain we have been using and the one that most neuroscientists seem to concentrate on is based on its physical structure.

The dicing and slicing of physical post-mortem specimens and **tomography** of the living, using MRI scanners, has resulted in great leaps in our understanding of the brain. The areas concerned with our five senses and our motor and autonomic functions are well known, as is the chemistry linked to both mood and the good and bad functioning of our psyche.

What remains elusive is the location of the mind and the mechanisms that generate self-awareness. Some neuroscientists shy away from this topic and leave it to the philosophers to debate.

So, in lieu of a scientific explanation for our consciousness and self awareness, we are left somewhat to our own devices to understand how the mind works. In the context of writer's block, of course, we are concerned about what stops the mind working and being creative.

To move forward in our understanding therefore, it's necessary to use a model for the mind which only has a loose scientific basis. What is amazing about adopting this model is that, especially in the field of creativity, great strides forward seem to be achievable.

Instead of slicing through the physical brain to look at its function, let's analyse the brain from a mind-ful perspective.

At the surface layer, we have what we call the conscious mind.

This gives us the illusion of reality, and also seems to have an in-built narrator which sometimes doubles up as an inner critic.

As you are reading these words and hopefully making some sense of them, try to identify who exactly is reading them and who is making sense of them?

To add a little further mystery, stop reading for a moment and listen to your inner voice. What accent is it speaking to you in?

Apparently it's been measured that the conscious mind can process about seven plus or minus two 'things' per second. This is probably why you can remember seven digit phone numbers and, if they are any bigger, you remember the area code as a chunk, like 020 or +00 31.

For much of the time, our conscious mind seems to be either idling or running an internal commentary of what we are *thinking*. Occasionally we can be replaying a previous encounter or previewing or planning something we are about to say in the future.

So it is your conscious mind which is probably *reading* these words to you. If so, consider who is reading what and to whom. If you have met me and know my voice, you may even superimpose it on the words as you read them. This is why I referred to as writing as a form of telepathy.

While all of this is going on, what is also feeding the conscious mind is the unconscious mind which is sometimes referred to as the subconscious mind. It is by definition everything we are potentially able to be conscious of but aren't particularly paying attention to at that time.

The unconscious mind primarily takes its input from your five senses of sight, hearing, taste, smell and touch. You will see later that this is not the limit of its inputs.

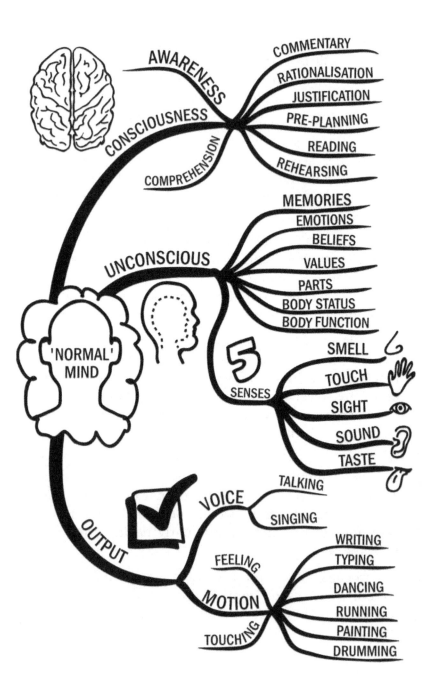

To show yourself how the unconscious mind works, think about your little finger. This will remind you that you have one. Or, have you ever noticed how you can pick out your name, or that of your favourite football team or rock band, from the background hubbub at a party?

The unconscious mind also regulates conveniently automated lower level functions such as breathing and your heart beat; you have to work a little to become aware of them and then to control them. Some functions such as blood sugar and hormone levels, for most, always remain in the subconscious domain.

Your unconscious mind is also both the seat of your emotions and the route to accessing all memories. It is said that it processes something like two million bits of information per second – a huge number but still probably a gross underestimate.

Whatever the number though, there is a huge gap between what the conscious and unconscious minds process.

What is clear is that certain types of mental activity block both the conscious and unconscious minds.

Try this. Get a piece of paper and a pen and start thinking of something. Then write it down and notice that at the point you start writing, the thinking seems to stop. When you stop writing, the thinking can start again. This demonstrates how we flip between thinking and doing. It's like you can only do one or the other. In fact, when you are writing, you almost become a reader.

Now repeat the same exercise but this time start thinking about how wonderful it would be for people to read and like your book. How great would it be to stop working and just earn a living from your book sales? All you would have to do is write and go to book signings. Notice that while you are having these thoughts how it is well nigh impossible to write. Now start writing anything and notice how the thoughts of your ego abate.

Can you also remember the last time you were pretty livid about something? Perhaps you had some road rage or a colleague did something to upset you at work. Imagine then if you had to write a chapter of your book or a sales presentation, your thoughts would keep flipping back to the source of your anger and away from the task in hand.

To be creative, your conscious and unconscious minds have to be not only uncluttered but also to be interacting in such a way to give clear access to your memories and inspirations.

What is actually happening is that our minds are constantly moving from one state of awareness and consciousness to another.

At the cusp between being conscious and unconscious, you are in a mode I call **Whole Mind Not-Thinking**. The trick for a writer is to get into this not-thinking state where the two minds are perfectly poised so that creativity can flow.

Meditation: A Tool For Whole Mind Not-Thinking

By far the best way to do this is to meditate regularly and, from such practice, to learn how to enter a wakeful meditative state while writing. The words and ideas will flow as if someone else is writing them.

For many people, the thought of meditating each day for twenty to thirty minutes sounds impossible, especially in an already busy day. I can testify though that your whole day will go much more smoothly and you will easily claw back this time. Meditation doesn't have to be something you do in a dark room with the lights off. You can meditate while walking or even commuting - ideally if someone else is driving. That said, if you have ever driven home and not been aware of how you got from A to B then you have already experienced a form of light meditative state. This is the mode you are aiming for while writing.

Perhaps you have tried meditating but have had trouble quietening the mind. Don't fret, this is quite normal. You can get hold of iPod-like meditation machines which can help induce the meditative state. These are brilliant for both novice and experienced meditators.

Most meditations use a device like a flame, a mantra or the breath as an external point to focus on to make thoughts go quiet. You can even use your footfalls in a walking meditation.

Which ever method works for you, feel free to use it; it is even better to use more than one, so you become adept at a variety of techniques.

Exercise 7: Collapsing Thoughts

> To augment this exercise you can listen to the
> 'Quantum Collapse of Thought' MP3 Visualisation.
> Details at the back of the book.

To allow you to experience and reproduce the meditative state on demand using thought itself as the point of focus, I'd like to introduce you to a technique I've called the **quantum collapse of thought**. This is loosely based on this quote that I read in a book called *The Self-Aware Universe* by Amit Goswami, from David Bohm and, before him, August Comte:

"If we concentrate on the content of thought, we lose sight of the direction in which the thought is heading. If we concentrate on the direction of a thought, we lose sharpness in its content."

I advocate that each writing session is preceded by a session of meditation. You will be amazed at how your words will start to flow.

You can do this exercise in two ways. Either listen to the *Quantum Collapse of Thought* in the MP3 Visualisation Pack or read the script below and work through it in your mind.

Sit upright in a chair with your back straight, your arms on your thighs and your feet uncrossed and flat on the floor. Optionally, you can use some light background instrumental music for this exercise

- Stare at the following image for 30-60 seconds.

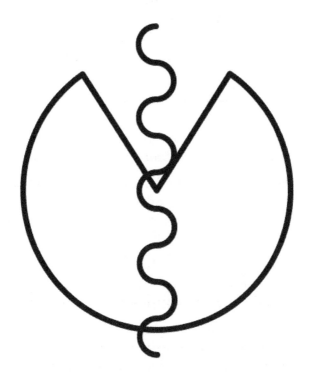

- Now close your eyes slowing and imagine a thin string pulling the crown of your head to the ceiling.

- Become aware of your breathing and, on the in breath, imagine your breath is rising from the base of your spine, up the outside of your spine to the top of your head.

- On the out breath, imagine it flows down the inside of your spine to the base.

- Do this nine times.

- Then let the tension flow out of your muscles, starting in your head, through your neck, down your arms, into your hands and out of your fingers.

- Now let the tension flow out of your chest, through your stomach, past your hips, down your thighs, through your calves and your ankles and out of your feet and toes into the floor.

- Become aware of your thoughts and where they are in your head – in the front for most people. As you refocus back on your breathing, observe your thoughts for a while.

- Notice you can ask them where they have come from and where they are going. You can also ask them to stop, turn around and go back.

- You can even start thinking your own thoughts about your thoughts which is kind of interesting. Who's doing the thinking and who's doing the observing? Do this for about a minute.

- Then put your tongue to the roof of your mouth and imagine a point an inch (2.5 cm) up and two inches (5 cm) back. This is where the pineal gland or third eye is sited.

- Now imagine your thoughts and consciousness moving from the front of your brain and moving back and shrinking down into the pineal gland.

- Focus back on your breathing for 30 seconds.

- With your consciousness at the centre of your brain, notice how you can look forward and *see* the backs of your eye sockets.

- Spend another few minutes observing your thoughts and mind from this position.

- When you are ready, open your eyes slowly and come back into your room. You may want to make notes of what you've experienced

This is an exercise you can do at anytime and pretty much anywhere once you are practiced at it. You can even use it when lying down if you want to get back to sleep in the early hours.

You will also see in the next chapters how to get your conscious and unconscious minds in balance and harmony. This allows you to tap into even higher states of mind which expand your reach and capability as a creative writer.

Tom Evans

CHAPTER 8

The Superconsciousness

*"Man's task is to become conscious
of the contents that press upward
from the unconscious."*

Carl Jung

Now we've started to think about the relationship between our mind and our thoughts, have you ever wondered where they come from ... and what they are made of and where they are going?

We take our thoughts for granted. We may never ask questions like this about them. It is said that, "Thoughts become things".

It is more accurate and useful to think of them *as* things. It is even more useful to imagine them as strings but that's the subject for a completely different book.

A writer who uses thoughts as a stock in trade will find it worthwhile paying more attention to what's going on in their grey matter.

Carl Jung, and many others before and since, postulated that there is something called the collective consciousness. It has many names such as the **cosmic consciousness, the Akashic Field, the Noosphere, the Morphic Field** and the **superconsciousness**. You will also find it called names like **Satori** and **Brahman** in theological and mystical literature. Some even refer to it as the 'mind of god'.

I make no such claims here and only refer to it in its usefulness as an unlimited resource for writers to tap into.

The concept of the superconsciousness, the term I prefer to use for its brevity and clarity, is quite attractive insofar as it seems to explain many everyday phenomena.

The idea is that all living, and non-living, things are connected in some way. Some physicists have theorised this happens in higher dimensions but the discussion of any mechanism is well outside the scope of this book. There is further reading on the subject at the back of this book if you are interested.

Have you ever thought of someone only for the 'phone to ring and to find it's them? Have you heard about those stories that dogs sense people are coming home? How did Leonardo da Vinci have the prescience to come up with the idea for both the helicopter and the parachute?

The superconsciousness is said to sit outside our time and space, acting as a storage mechanism for all thoughts, feelings, wisdom and knowledge.

If this is true, the very thoughts you and I are having now are passing to and from the superconsciousness. Every man, woman and child (and animal and plant) that ever lived is also tapped into it. This also includes versions of you and me in the future and the past.

In terms of *the you in the past,* it could explain how we retrieve memories, or not. As for tapping into *the you in the future,* this would explain so-called psychic phenomenon such as precognition. Actually, when you hyphenate words, you get to understand their true meaning so, for example, pre-science and pre-cognition indicate their underlying meaning.

If you then extrapolate this idea, there must be a version of you, and your readers, in the future who have read the words you haven't written yet. How useful would it be if you could connect with that person? This would spell the end of writer's block for ever.

Well, if you haven't been left behind with the farfetchedness of all of this, the key to tapping into the superconsciousness is accessing the meditative state while Whole Mind Not-thinking. Getting the left and right hemispheres in synchronisation while Whole Brain Thinking was a bit of a warm up.

We need to extend the model a little and introduce the idea that there is a layer of our mind which sits between the unconscious mind and the superconsciousness.

This layer of mind is again one that instinctively we feel we possess. It has many names but we will call it the **Higher Self**. You could equally call it the Lower Self, the Inner Self or the Outer Self. This is because it sits outside our normal three space and one time dimensions and is the part of our mind that connects us with the superconsciousness.

The Higher Self can also be thought of as a part of us that acts as a guide, directing us through our life experiences, both good and bad.

If you accept that the superconsciousness stores all thoughts, this could explain how sometimes you have an idea and don't act on it only to see someone else come out with your invention a year or so later. How annoying is that?

Shown here is a two dimensional representation of how this type of occurrence could come about. You will notice how the conscious mind is surrounded by the unconscious mind which in turn is enveloped by the Higher Self. The route to the superconsciousness is via the unconscious mind, and the Higher Self is the connector.

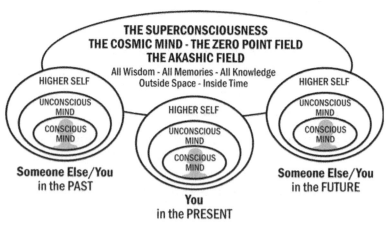

It could be that your idea leaks out into the superconsciousness. Just as likely, more than one person taps into the idea at the same time, but only one carries it through to completion. For all I know, someone else is writing a book just like this on writer's block at this very moment.

I cannot stress enough that whether all this exists or not is academic, and it is not the aim of this book to begin to explain or prove or disprove it. What is remarkable is that just by thinking, or more accurately not-thinking, in this way works wonders for a writer.

Using these concepts, our minds can be tuned into previously hidden inspiration. As you will see later, this can be considerably enhanced by something else we all do naturally, breathing.

Exercise 8: Tuning in

The superconscious also relays information to us in many ways. Sometimes it comes as thoughts but it also uses all the other five senses or versions of them.

You may have heard of the sixth sense. Well there are at least six sixth senses. Try saying that quickly.

They are:

- Clairvoyance – vision
- Clairaudience – hearing
- Clairgustatory – taste
- Clairolfactory – smell
- Clairsentience – feeling
- Claircogniscence – knowing

A full treatment of how to enhance each of these is outside the scope of this book but it is worth mentioning that your connection to the superconsciousness will use all of them. As for the normal five senses, people are more sensitive in some more than the others.

We'll deal just with the latter in this next exercise, namely **claircogniscence** and the thought forms that emanate from the superconsciousness. In the further reading section at the back of the book, you will find books that will help you with the others.

In your head you will now have any number of thoughts milling around. So how can you differentiate between your own thoughts and those that have come from the superconsciousness? Well it's a process of elimination.

As you are reading this book, your conscious mind is actually reading the words. If you are thinking about a conversation you had yesterday or a speech you are giving tomorrow, then your conscious mind is in operation. Have a 'listen to your thoughts right now.

If while you are reading this book, you feel a bit peckish or get a warm feeling of an awoken memory or sense a dull ache somewhere in your body, this is your unconscious mind at work.

Your unconscious mind also operates about half a second to a second ahead of the conscious mind. This explains many, but not all, of those incidences when you know the phone is about to ring, and who is on the other end, just before it does.

You will see in the next chapter how the information from the unconscious mind can be classified still further and used to extend your sensory powers as a writer.

If you are suddenly reminded you must make a phone call or pay a bill, this is your Higher Self at work. Perhaps you were about to pull out at a T-junction in your car and suddenly stopped only to miss a previously unseen motorcycle by inches. Your Higher Self is silently protecting you. By the way, it likes to be thanked so do so if this ever happens to you.

If anything else comes in, this is more than likely a thought form from the superconsciousness. A telltale sign is the classic light bulb moment where you get a whole image, from nowhere, in less than a second.

What's more, these moments happen when your conscious and unconscious mind are quiet. When you are in deep meditation or just while you are driving or listening to ambient music. They don't tend to happen when your internal dialogue is running or if you are flushed with a strong emotion like road rage.

If you ignore the messages from the superconsciousness, you often get reminded and the reminders might not just come as thoughts. You may see something on TV or in a newspaper or an advertisement.

Car number plates can also be a rich source of communication but that's a different story.

The following image shows a more comprehensive model for our minds, which incorporates not only our five senses but also all the other input we are bombarded with, when awake or asleep.

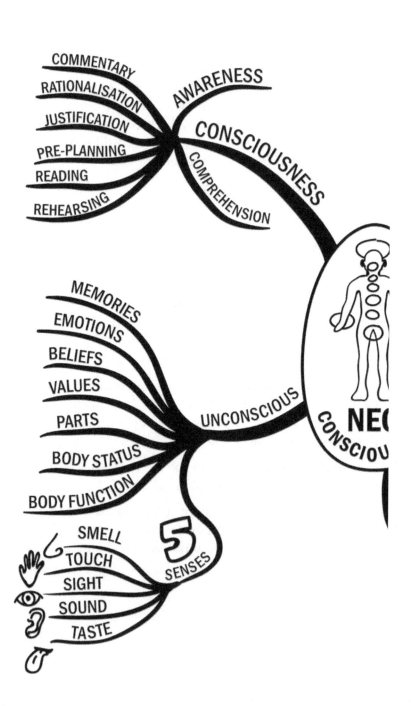

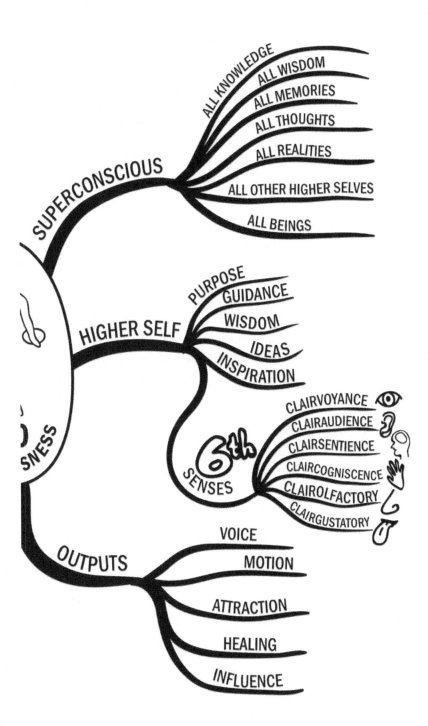

For this next exercise, all you need to do is to spend a little time considering the different types of thoughts mentioned in this chapter, and start to generate an awareness of their different flavours. For people with strong clairaudience, these thought forms actually come in strongly as a voice either right inside the brain or sometimes just behind an ear. Those who are clairvoyant will see images.

Most people are both clairvoyant and clairaudient and experience examples nightly but this is often not recognised for what it is. When you dream, you are in direct communication with the higher consciousnesses. You will see later how to tap into this so you can literally write whole chapters on demand while you are sleeping.

Every single person has the ability to either ignore or tune into this full gamut of sensibility. Your task is to become acquainted with your super-senses and to learn how invaluable they are to a writer. To do so allows you move into a new expanded state of mind, sometimes referred to as the **neo-consciousness**.

CHAPTER 9

Becoming Fear-less

"The components of anxiety, stress, fear, and anger do not exist independently of you in the world. They simply do not exist in the physical world, even though we talk about them as if they do."

Wayne Dyer

An intimate relationship with your unconscious mind leads to amazing results.

Apart from allowing us to carry out complex tasks, like driving or typing, while the conscious mind is free to think, the unconscious mind is also our protector. It will naturally steer us away from trouble, sometimes without us being consciously aware of it.

In the context of writing a book, if you don't write it, you can't be ridiculed. If you don't get it published, you can't fail. You will never know what it would have been like to be a successful author and you won't take your life into uncharted territory.

You will never have to face these deep fears which can stop us from writing.

They are established as patterns, also known as gestalts, in our unconscious mind to protect us. Sometimes they are installed by accident or carelessly.

Perhaps a teacher criticised an essay or told you to stop dreaming about being an artist or astronaut. Your parents may have encouraged you to get a proper career or vocation as a plumber, a lawyer or a doctor and told you that there's no money in the arts.

We need to be very careful what we say to children.

From a creative perspective, harbouring fears can have a disastrous effect. In the diagram below, you can see how the conscious mind connects with the higher self and then through to the superconsciousness – the source of inspiration.

Collective Consciousness via Higher Self

Unconscious Mind

NEGATIVE EMOTIONS & PAINFUL MEMORIES OR EXPERIENCES

Anger | Sadness | Fear | Hurt | Guilt

Conscious Mind

YOUR THINKING | INNER CRITIC
INNER DIALOGUE | YOUR EGO

Blocks

If you are experiencing negative emotions such as fear or anger, this will block any attempt at creativity. You can see also in this diagram how conscious thought processes also block the creative flow.

That said, as a creative writer, we may need to access our fears so we can write about them, and induce them telepathically in our readers.

Some conventional therapies focus on deletion of negative emotions. While this can be beneficial in the short term, what is really needed is the ability to access these emotions yet remain detached from the physical association caused by being in the state they normally induce.

The only sure fire way to address fears is to embrace them and face them head on.

For example, if you want to swim the Channel but haven't learned to swim, a good place to start would be in the local swimming baths. It would be a good idea to start in the shallow end with some buoyancy aids and be with someone who can already swim. After some time, you can lose the aids, swim a width and venture into the deep end by yourself.

The same is true of creative writing. If you look back at the exercises in chapters one to three you will see they all focus on getting your writing feet wet.

There will come a time when you are working on the first draft of your first book and old fears surface that stop you finishing it. The fears themselves might not even be in your conscious awareness.

The sign that this is going on is that you busy yourself doing anything other than writing and finishing those last crucial chapters of your book.

You may find you are busy helping other people before you, or bury yourself in household chores or a mound of paperwork. See this as a symptom not the cause, although you, or external agencies, may make it seem so.

It is time to access the fears that are stopping you and to take full charge of the writing process. Only you can finish your book, not your boss, your partner or your colleagues or children. They may all belong to the great mass of the not-written and not-published.

Exercise 9: Becoming Fear-less

> To augment this exercise you can listen to
> the 'Becoming Fear-Less' MP3 Visualisation.
> Details at the back of the book.

As children we may have been fearful of many things - a scary story or thunder and lightning. As adults we learn that we don't need to fear lightning but its wise not to stand on the top of a hill holding a long metal spike.

We learn to overcome and understand our fears.

For a writer, there are four main fears to address:

- Fear of unknown
- Fear of failure
- Fear of ridicule
- Fear of success

By far the best way to address all of these is to take small steps to overcome them. Write a short story (perhaps in Six Sentences), publish it online or send it into a competition. Join a local writing group. Oddly enough, joining a reading group is also really useful, as you can study how published authors go about their craft.

The feedback you get from publishing and sharing your work will either give you confidence or inform you that there is more you need to learn.

Imagine you had to jump out of a crashing aeroplane, with a parachute, to save your life. It might not be the best most comfortable option but you would probably do it. This is because the fear of jumping is less than the fear of crashing.

Let's take this analogy and apply it to the questions below:

Fear of The Unknown

- What don't you know?
- What would you like to know?
- How would you feel if you knew what you didn't know that you want to know?

Fear of Failure

- What would failure look like to you?
- What would the benefit of failing be?
- What might you learn from failing?

Fear of Ridicule

- Who are you most afraid of?
- Has this happened before? If so, when and how did you react?
- What would you like to be able to say to someone who ridicules you?

Fear of Success

- What image of success are you fearful of?
- What would a successful success look like?
- What steps can you take to make (a) into (b)?

When you have finished answering these questions you may want to listen to *Becoming Fear-less* in the MP3 Visualisation Pack.

CHAPTER 10

Vestigial Minds

"Nature begins to whisper its secrets to us through its sounds. Sounds that were previously incomprehensible to our soul now become the meaningful language of nature."

Rudolf Steiner

If you did biology at school, you may have heard about **vestigial organs**. These are parts of our anatomy we used in our evolutionary past which have now atrophied to a remnant. Examples include the skin flap in the lower corner of our eye near our nose and the appendix.

You have heard and used phrases like, "It's on the tip of my tongue" or "My heart goes out to you." We talk about how we can feel it in our water or that your gut tells you something. Our language gives much away about what is really going on in our minds, and our bodies.

There is a conventional view that the complexity of the human brain generates self-awareness.

As we have evolved, the frontal lobes of our brain have taken on the very onerous role of processing not only our thoughts but our feelings. This is why you can sometimes be in two minds over something, with your heart telling you one thing and your head the other. Alternatively, you may find yourself saying, "I think I'll go with my gut on this one."

These utterances are no accident.

They are a reflection of what is actually going on in your body.

Our minds inhabit every cell of our body, and quite possibly outside our physical form. Our brains act a sort of central processing unit that generates the illusion of reality based on the input from our primary, and sixth, senses. Its function is to process and to allow us to think and express ourselves.

At various points in our body we have conglomerations of aspects of our minds centred on areas like the larynx, the heart and the gut. These are just the three of the most well known points in and around our bodies known as **chakras**. They are like portals to different aspects of the superconsciousness and we have over two hundred of them.

Any such metaphysical discussion is way beyond the scope of this book and I stress that these ideas are only concepts to allow us to become better, and more prolific, writers.

As mentioned earlier, the brain exhibits a phenomenon called plasticity. If an area of the brain is damaged, say in a stroke, mechanisms come into play to rewire neural pathways around the damaged areas. Both physical and mental exercises help to speed up this process. We can use this principle to expand and nurture our minds into new ways of thinking and being.

Just doing this regularly seems to be enough to make the change occur. The exercises in this book are all designed with this in mind. When you picked up this book, you may have had a mental pattern that resulted in a creative blockage. As you complete exercises that are perhaps new to you, new pathways are formed.

This next step could be one of the most vital you ever take in tapping into your full creative flow and that's to re-engage with your vestigial mind centres.

It turns out that these centres are much better adapted to processing certain types of thoughts than our brains. When we engage with them not only do we tap into a rich vein of material for a book but the brain becomes unencumbered and we begin to think much more clearly. Naturally this has benefits in all aspects of life.

This whole subject merits a book in its own right and to keep this simple to understand, we will concern ourselves with just four of the most useful centres within the body at this stage. We will also explore one centre which exists just outside the body too.

Starting with a lower point in our body, somewhere just around the navel, is the location of our gut mind. This is the area where we generate our drive and desire to move forward. It is referred to as the **solar plexus chakra** and is where we generate the fuel for our body. You may often pat it after a good meal. It is also the area best suited to processing thoughts relating to instincts.

Learning to trust this, in preference to your editor or even your readers, is a real essential for any writer. It will direct you to the best title for your book, the chapter structure, the words to use and the connections you need to make for your book to be published, to sell and become a success.

Next is our heart centre, or **heart chakra**, which unsurprisingly is the location for our feelings and emotions. It provides a rich source of material for your writing and is also a great place to get feedback on the quality of what you are producing.

You can get a warm feeling in your chest that resonates with the words you are writing and these feelings are in turn picked up by the reader. If you are harbouring doubts or fears, your heart centre is eminently more suited to dealing with them than your brain. Quite literally, this is the place to tap into when you really want to love what you are doing.

The next centre is located around our larynx and this is the area from which we speak and communicate with the outside world. It is also known as your **throat chakra**. One useful way of proof reading anything you have written is to read it out loud. If it comes across clearly to your ears, it will read well. If you find you are pausing for breath then you should look at punctuation and sentence structure.

The last centre within our body is the **third eye** or **pineal gland**, which is located pretty much in the centre of our brains at the top of the spinal column. This is the place within our bodies where we receive our intuition and inspiration. Learning to listen to it and trust it is essential for anyone engaged in the creative process.

Finally, imagine a point an inch or above your head. This somewhat ethereal point is known as the **alpha chakra** and it's thought to be the place where your brain-mind connects with the superconsciousness. I cannot stress enough that it doesn't matter if this is all physically true but, you will make huge leaps forward by merely thinking that it is.

The proof, if needed, is in the pudding of your creative output.

In summary, you have within, and without, you dormant areas that you can use as an unlimited creative resource.

Your gut can be relied upon to direct you.

Your heart can tap into for source material and for feedback on how you feel. It will also handle and process your fears.

Your voice allows you to check your words are *re-sounding*. The use of the hyphen here is intentional.

Your third eye is the communication channel to your conscious mind for the inspiration provided to you by the superconsciousness via your alpha chakra.

Now this might all sound fantastical or even confusing. How do you go about using these mind centres? How do you know which one is talking to you and which one to trust?

The next exercise will help you engage with them, but one of the most useful ways is to analyse your own language. By your own language, I refer to your body language, your spoken and written words and your internal dialogue. They are your barometers.

Let me give you some examples.

If you ever see me speak, you will often see me grasp the air above my head. I had no idea I did this until it was pointed out to me by a lady who can see auras. She saw me pulling ideas out of the ether into my brain.

Notice where you place your hands when you speak. Sometimes, you pat your chest or hold them over your neck or on your forehead. It is because you are working primarily with that mind centre.

Listen to others when they say things like, "Let's sound this out." They are using their larynx centre to test an idea.

If you have just typed something that really warms you and creates a feeling of love, or sadness, you can be sure this has come straight from the heart.

At the end of reading this chapter, which I know might sound a bit *out there*, you may want to give your left, analytical brain a rest. Just ask yourself, what does your gut tell you about all this? Is it at least worth investigating and trying out?

Is it possible that writer's block becomes a thing of the past when you set all your minds to work on what you are writing? Who knows? As I said at the start of this book, it's an exploration, and the next exercise is designed for you to start a dialogue with your vestigial minds.

Exercise 10: Re-Minding Yourself

To augment this exercise you can listen to the
'Re-Minding Yourself' MP3 Visualisation.
Details at the back of the book.

What is so wonderful about the brain and the mind is that the patterns we build up which don't serve us can be so easily replaced by ones that do. You may have heard it said, "If something doesn't work, then try something else until it does."

Marketing is a great example of that.

In the last exercise, you explored how different types of thoughts appear to us. We will explore this further now by looking at the various flavours of conscious thought. By reconnecting with your vestigial minds you achieve three feats at once:

- Your conscious brain frees up for pure thought
- You become more efficient
- Your vestigial minds become a rich source of material for you as a writer

Before you do the next exercise, which you may want to do in private, stare at the following image for 30-60 seconds.

Now go inside yourself and think about you and the book you would like to write. Get a Post It note pad and tear off four notes.

1. On the first note, list as many of the *goals* as you can think of that you would like to achieve from writing the book – both as an author, in your business or career and in your personal life.

2. On the second note, write down all the *feelings* being a successful author invokes in you – both positive and negative.

3. Now imagine yourself at a book signing reading a chapter from your book. Write down, on the third note, the opening line of what you would like to say in your introductory talk.

4. On the last note, write down your idea for the title of your book.

Now stick the first note to your clothing just around your navel. You may need additional sticky tape.

Stick the second note in the middle of your chest.

Stick the third note on your neck.

Stick the fourth note on your forehead.

You may think this a bit silly but trust me, it works. They don't have to stay there for long!

Now stare at the following image for 60 seconds and when you are done, take the notes off. You may then want to stick them on a note board with the fourth at the top and the first at the bottom to re-mind yourself some more.

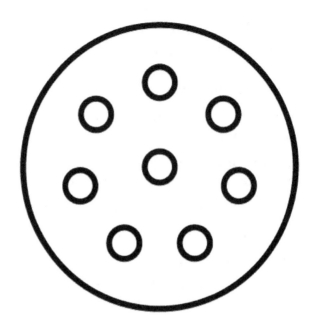

When you have finished you may also like to listen to *Re-Minding Yourself* in the MP3 Visualisation Pack.

As you will see in the remaining chapters, by reconnecting to your vestigial minds, you start to become whole and inspired, yet immensely grounded.

You enter a state of **neo-consciousness**.

CHAPTER 11

The Physicality Of Inspiration

"All the principles of heaven and earth are living inside you. Life itself is truth, and this will never change. Everything in heaven and earth breathes. Breath is the thread that ties creation together."

Morihei Ueshiba

The brain is about two per cent of the adult total body weight but consumes something like 25% of the energy from our bodies. It also burns about 25% of the body's nutrients and it is estimated it takes 70% of the glucose we consume.

This is one reason we can faint to protect ourselves, as I mentioned earlier, and you can become mentally exhausted if you are thinking and processing too many things. This is, of course, where using your vestigial minds really comes into its own.

It might come as no surprise that with all this new brain and mind activity, it is a good idea to pay attention to our fuel intake.

It's natural when you are embarking on a journey to make sure you have enough food and liquid to sustain you – or have the means - a credit card perhaps - to get what you need. A creative writing journey is no different. What you take into your body dramatically affects how we perform as anyone who has ever been inebriated will testify.

While food is an obvious form of energy, you have been providing your brain with lots of energy already through many of the exercises in this book by simply breathing.

Another reason why breathing and paying particular attention to your breath is important is to do with how and when thoughts to appear from the superconsciousness.

If you look up the word inspiration in a dictionary, you will see the following definitions:

1. An inspiring or animating action or influence

2. Something inspired, as an idea

3. A result of inspired activity

4. A thing or person that inspires

5. Theology:
     a. a divine influence directly and immediately exerted upon the mind or soul
     b. the divine quality of the writings or words of a person so influenced

6. The drawing of air into the lungs; inhalation

The first four you will probably have expected but it's maybe a surprise to see that there is a fifth theological connotation for inspiration.

The last definition is one that most people don't think of even though it's perhaps fairly obvious. Inspiration is one half of the respiration process.

Further insight comes from its etymology, or root meaning. The word inspiration is comprised of the word *in* and the Latin *spirare*, to breathe.

We speak on the out breath. Could it be therefore that ideas come to us on the in breath?

Eastern mystical practices such as **Taoism** use breathing exercises in meditation to balance **Yin** and **Yang** energies and encourage the connection to the divine.

The visualisations in this book work in the same way. You are encouraged to breathe in from the base of your spine to the top of your head and down again.

You can enhance the effectiveness of this breathing pattern by imagining that ideas and wisdom are coming in on the in breath and then thanking the superconsciousness (or the universe or your god or guardian angels) on the out breath.

This technique also draws the inspiration past all your vestigial mind centres which allows the idea to come in different forms. You may get it directly in the third eye point as knowledge, or it can come in as a gut instinct or a heart felt feeling. The clairaudient can receive actual words.

Once you master the art of right breathing, you will find you start to use your diaphragm much more.

Practices such as **Pilates, Qi Gong** and **Tai Chi** are recommended for anyone engaged in the creative arts.

The next things to focus on are the nutrients carried by the oxygenated blood the brain and, of course, all the internal vestigial mind centres. The exercise in this chapter is all about eating the right food for thought. Even with the best food intake, it is vital that the blood is well oxygenated to deliver maximum benefit to the brain.

Exercise 11: Food For Thought

Research has shown that there is a connection between what we eat and how we feel. The biochemical basis of this food-mood link lies in the chemical messengers, called **neurotransmitters**, that relay thoughts and actions along the neural pathways of the brain.

As food affects the action of these chemical messengers it can also have an impact on our mood. Nutrient choice is therefore important to support the thought process. Meal timing, portion sizes and the combination of foods, play a vital role in the regulation of mood and energy. They influence blood-sugar levels which can leave us as high as a kite one minute and scrambling through the cupboard the next, in search of a sugar fix

For this next exercise, look at how your food affects your creative performance. Like many of the exercises in this book, the benefits to be had by this approach will have an impact on other areas in your life.

Go Low Glycemic

Carbohydrates, in particular, affect our energy levels and mood. High sugar products raise blood sugar for a short period, always followed by a dip that leaves you unfocused and lethargic.

Low-glycemic carbohydrates (e.g. brown rice, pasta, vegetables), on the other hand, provide more stable energy and mood levels. Small portions of complex carbohydrate at regular intervals throughout the day will be effective in regulating energy.

Glycemic Index (GI) refers to the rate at which sugar from a particular food enters the cells of the body. Foods with a high glycemic index stimulate the pancreas to secrete insulin, quickly emptying sugar from the blood into the cells. This produces the familiar ups and downs of blood sugar and the roller coaster energy levels that go with it. Foods with a lower glycemic index do not push the pancreas to secrete so much insulin, so blood sugar tends to be steadier. Eating low GI foods and combining carbohydrate with protein and fibre will reduce the rate at which sugar empties into the cells.

You should, therefore, combine low GI carbohydrates, protein and vegetables or fruit in each meal or snack sitting. Some good examples are:

- Chicken, brown rice and roasted vegetables

- Salmon, couscous and greens

- Wholemeal pitta with tuna and salad

- Nuts and fruit

- Wholemeal cereal and semi-skimmed milk with fruit

Meal Patterns

The most effective way to keep energy level even across the day is to spread your calorie need over five to six small meals, rather than the traditional three. This can help you avoid the commonly experienced mid-morning and mid-afternoon energy dips that leave you lacking concentration and focus.

Unsurprisingly, the most common time for people to visit the office vending machine is mid-afternoon, as those who have not eaten a healthy lunchtime snack are on a mission to get a sugar-fix.

Prepare some healthy snacks in the morning so that your work-flow is not interrupted when you sit down to write, and think carefully about which nutrients you select for a brain boosting breakfast, lunch and dinner.

Foods With The Best Brain Balance

Fruit such as grapefruit, apples, cherries, oranges and grapes have a lower glycemic index. Fruit has a lower GI than fruit juice, because the fibre in the fruit slows the absorption of the fruit sugar. A whole apple will therefore be more brain friendly than apple juice.

For cereals and grains, oatmeal and bran have the lowest GI. Other foods with a favourable GI include spaghetti and brown rice. Corn flakes and sugar-coated cereals have a high GI and are therefore not ideal.

Vegetables, soybeans, kidney beans, chickpeas and lentils have the lowest glycemic index of any food. White potatoes have quite a high GI so try to opt for sweet potato instead.

Finally dairy products, milk and yoghurt have a low GI, slightly higher than vegetables but lower than fruit. Plain yoghurt has a lower glycemic index than flavoured yoghurts with added sugar.

Happy Foods

During the winter months we are starved of sunlight and this can lead to a reduction in the release of **serotonin**, an important chemical found in the brain. Serotonin is referred to as the *feel good* hormone and reduction in its release can lead to the development of serious seasonal depression for some, or just a dip in mood for others. Interestingly, our food intake also has an impact on the release of this hormone and tweaking our diets can lead to an improvement in mood, or halt this dip altogether.

Particular foods have a calming effect on the body that results in heightened feelings of happiness. Chocolate can have this effect as it triggers the release of serotonin and endorphins that make us feel good. Other happy foods include chicken, milk, leafy green vegetables and bananas which all contain a compound called **tryptophan**.

Tryptophan is an amino acid and one of the building blocks of protein. It competes for access to the central nervous system, with several other amino acids, and it is thought to increase the brain's production of serotonin, and subsequently to elevate mood.

It is known as Nature's Prozac.

Perky Foods

Proteins in the diet affect brain performance, either leaving us alert and productive or ready for bed. Rich foods can make us feel alert, jumpstarting the brain so we are ready for action.

Another amino acid that increases neurotransmitter activity is **Tyrosine**. High tyrosine foods include seafood, soy, meat, beans, tofu and eggs; eating them can leave you focused and motivated.

Essential Fatty Acids

Essential fatty acids (**EFAs**) also play a role in mood regulation. Those with low intakes of Omega 3 fatty acids have been found to be more likely to experience Seasonal Affective Disorder (**SAD**) during the winter months. Three to six grammes of EFAs - taken in the form of food like fish, avocado, nuts or supplements - are recommended for general health and mood promotion.

Water, Water Everywhere

Drinking enough water will also make a dramatic improvement to energy levels. Aim to sip on small glasses of water throughout the day. If you don't want to interrupt your train of thought by nipping into the kitchen to re-fill your glass, fill a litre sports drink bottle and sip one over each half of the day.

Copy out the image on the next page and put it underneath your water glass and it will energise the molecules of water and, of course, you.

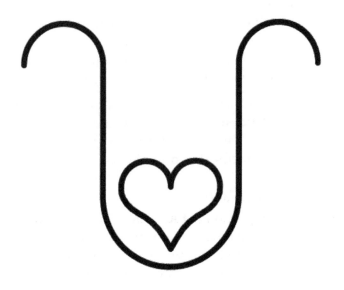

CHAPTER 12

Using Dreamtime

"Eventually we learn how to connect these higher sleep experiences with our ordinary sense-perceptible surroundings."

Rudolph Steiner

Apart from being able to recharge your cells, wouldn't it be great to use the seven or eight hours every day when we're sleeping to benefit your writing?

This is especially useful when you have been engaging new parts of your brain, and body. After the mental exercises in this book, you may find you need a bit of a rest and that you start to sleep much better and sounder.

This is fortunate as dreams are a rich source of information for writers, musicians and artists. Scientists too have inspirational dreams.

Apocryphally, the German biochemist Kekulé had a dream about a snake devouring its tail. From this vision, he made the conscious mind leap that organic compounds could assemble in circles. He came up with the **benzene ring** from which came the basis for all organic chemistry.

When we are dreaming, we are in a timeless state. A dream that lasts for a few minutes can seem to us, upon awakening, to have lasted for an hour or more. When we are dreaming, it feels as real as our normal awakened state. Both are illusions of one kind or another.

When we dream, we are pretty much in direct communication with the superconsciousness.

You may also hear it said that you are connected with the **ethereal** and **astral planes** when you are dreaming. People also report out of body experiences, known as **OBEs**.

I have always had the theory since my childhood that one part of the dream sequence is you uploading stuff that happened in the day. Another aspect is you downloading information that could be useful to you. The dreams themselves are the story that an aspect of our consciousness makes up to rationalise it all.

There are many different sleep states but the most memorable and vivid ones are known as **lucid dreams**. It is possible for us to influence their direction and ask for specific guidance on our writing.

Using dreams as source material might daunt you especially if you have trouble remembering them. This next exercise is designed to help and it uses as its premise the tendency for most memorable dreams to be those you have just before waking.

Apocryphally Salvador Dali used to put a spoon under his elbow around siesta time. We he nodded off and it clattered to the floor, he'd awaken and paint what was on his mind. It's said that the great inventor - or is that in-venter? - Thomas Edison used a similar trick with a metal bowl and some glass marbles.

Exercise 12: Remembering & Interpreting Dreams

The best way to remember your dreams is to be in the same state you were in when you had them – i.e. semi-sleep.

The most memorable dreams are those you have just before waking. The point between waking and sleeping is eloquently known as the **hypnagogic** state.

The point between sleeping and waking is known as the **hypnopompic** state. This is the one that matters. It is the most useful to anyone trying to remember their dreams.

To make best use of this hypnopompic state you should stay in it as long as possible. This is quite a nice thing to treat yourself to anyway.

You should try and wake up slowly and let the dream filter into your conscious mind. Then in your note pad, write down just the bullet points and main essence of the dream, not the whole story.

If it is important and you can't get back to sleep, you can do this in the middle of the night too.

Next comes the analysis of the dream itself although sometimes the message in the dream is so obvious you may not need to do this.

I don't advise you read a dream interpretation book, as this is someone else's view of what dreams mean, not yours.

To analyse a dream, you need to make a couple of leaps of imagination, and disassociation.

Draw a table with three columns.

1. Put the bullets points of your dream in the first column.

2. In the second column, write down what else it could mean. Be inventive and abstract.

3. In the third column, write down what the thought in the second (not the first column) could mean in the context of your book.

You can also seed your dream with a request for your next chapter before you go to sleep. Ask your unconscious mind to ask your Higher Self for a dream that will be useful to you.

You can even write your request on a bit of paper and put it under your pillow. I know it might sound silly, but it works and takes little effort to try.

Note that accurate and useful dream analysis is something that comes with practice - you will be amazed at the insights you receive.

CHAPTER 13

Reader-Centric Writing

"A reader is not supposed to be aware that someone's written the story. He's supposed to be completely immersed, submerged in the environment."

Jack Vance

I am sure you have read articles or books where you got the impression that the writer is intent on showing you how clever they are. Every sentence is perhaps littered with a word that makes you reach for the dictionary.

On the other hand, we have all read a book that we couldn't put down? We just had to read the next chapter even though we should really have gone to sleep with a busy day ahead.

In the same way that rampant emotions can interrupt our creative flow at the level of the unconscious mind, the ego can wreak creative havoc at a conscious mind level if it engages while you are writing.

Not only will the reader spot it straight away but you will be writing from the conscious mind and will find it hard to engage with your own emotions, or those of your reader.

Consider this example:

"I stood on the burning deck. The flames were licking at my feet now and I could smell my nasal hairs burning. I was between a big rock and a really hard place. If I jumped into the water, the sharks would have me in minutes. Hang on, is that a helicopter I can hear?"

Imagine that this was the opening sentence to a chapter you were writing. Perhaps it's a story about the hijacking of a ship or a spy novel. Note that it's written in the first person from the perspective of the person trapped in the fire.

Close your eyes and imagine how horrific this would be. Go inside and feel which of your vestigial minds is most active. Your heart will be pounding and your brain will be crying out subliminally to your gut for help and guidance.

Now put yourself in the position of the helicopter pilot. Your training means you have to be calm and collected at these times. You know you have loads of fuel on board as well as an excellent winch operator and medic. You are confident that you will easily be able to rescue the person on deck and have them in hospital back on land within 20 minutes. What is going on your mind? You will be no doubt focused on the job in hand.

Next imagine you are a shark. You have already smelt a molecule of blood that has dropped into the sea. You have no idea about the turmoil going on above the water, not least what fire is, yet your primeval instincts sense a meal could be coming your way. One of your brains has told your stomach to start secreting digestive juices. If you were a land animal, the slobber might be visible from your mouth.

So with one simple premise in a single sentence, that of someone in some trouble, you can completely change the point and direction of the story.

This book is not about creative writing *per se* but this is a great example of how to easily get around a block in your writing. Simply look at what you are writing about from another point of view.

The example above is fictional so it allows for a large amount of creative freedom but the same applies to non-fiction books. For example, I could have written this book in the first person singular giving you an account of how I go about writing and getting over blocks. Now I am a fairly modest chap but even I would have struggled to keep my ego at bay if had done so.

I could have equally written it in the third person by writing, "the author does this ..." or "one encounters that ..." which could have been dry or seen as a bit of a text book treatment.

Instead, I have written it primarily in the second person with occasional forays into the first person such as this.

I have been careful to use language that is easy to understand and any complex terms or new words are explained. The last thing I want to do when writing a book on writer's block is to put any barriers in the way.

You will also note each chapter is relatively short as are the sentences and paragraphs.

I also used the techniques advocated in the book while writing it. Before I wrote each chapter, I meditated. I have been mindful of my breath and have been watching what I am eating and drinking.

If I got stuck, and I did, I went out for a walk for some inspiration.

Finally, each chapter ends with a simple exercise which gives the reader additional information and a chance to integrate the learnings such as this next one.

Exercise 13: Profiling Your Reader

I came across a term recently called vanity publishing. This is where the only aim for the author was to see their name on the front of a book. It differs from other forms of publication insofar as the main aim is solely to get in print with a few copies for themselves and their family and friends.

If you have higher aspirations than this and you want your book to sell, you have to get inside the mind of your reader and perhaps carry out some market research.

For this exercise, start a new Mind Map to profile your reader.

On your map, draw a branch and add the age range of your reader.

Draw another and list what percentage is male or female.

Are you aiming at a particular demographic slice of the population?

You may even find it useful to put names of people you know into the map so when you started writing you use words and concepts you know that they will understand.

Next describe what they like, including details like their political and sexual persuasion and what books they will like. Try and make them relevant to your book.

Finally, describe the impact reading your book will have on them.

What will they now think?

What will they feel and what action will they take?

The reason this is so vital is that the legacy that your book leaves in peoples' minds is probably more important than how they felt when reading the book itself.

Hopefully they will tell all their friends to buy a copy.

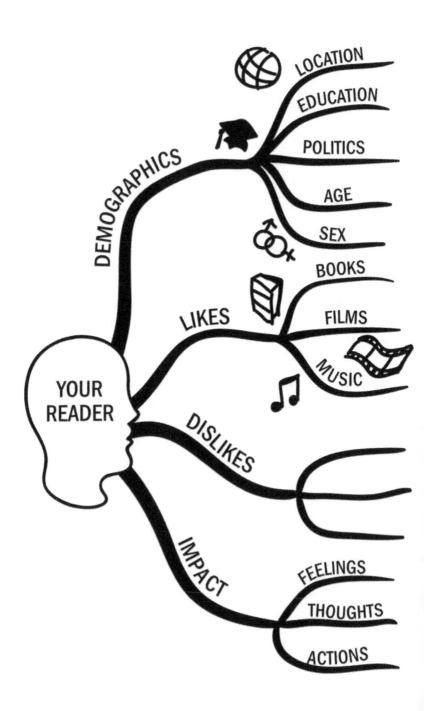

CHAPTER 14

Expanding Time

"We have come to see time as the enemy – as something that's always racing away from us. And we spend too much of it focusing on the past and the future."

Steve Taylor, author of *Making Time*

You may have found yourself wishing there were more hours in a day.

You may have been stuck in an airport lounge or a railway station when a plane or train is late and perhaps you had nothing to read. Do you remember how time can drag?

Perhaps at a party when you met loads of new people and had a fabulous time? Before you know it, it's the *witching hour* and your taxi's arrived to take you home.

Time is very subjective and a product of our conscious mind. Herein lies the key into creating more of it.

If your conscious mind is active when you are writing, it will have the effect of speeding up time. Conversely, if it is suppressed, time seems to expand.

The trick for a writer, or any artist, is to get in the zone. This is a timeless mode where you seem to get four or more hours work done in an hour. The words just flow and the outside world disappears from your consciousness.

You become one with the words you are typing and they flow off your pen or on to your computer screen.

What's more, the words will make sense next to each other, with each paragraph flowing logically into the next. If you are writing dialogue, you are there in the scene with your characters perhaps even speaking one or more parts of the dialogue with your inner voice.

You give yourself up to the words and you know they are just perfect and meant to be. When you finish writing you feel a great sense of achievement, pride and even catharsis. You have downloaded something that has been 'at the back of your mind' or 'a weight on your chest'. You can now move onwards and upwards.

You look at the clock and wonder where the time went.

An unexpected bonus is that, as you write in a trance-like state, you unconsciously write words that enable your reader to empathetically enter a similar state.

With a little study and planning, you also can learn how to consciously entrance your reader. This is something great storytellers, and stand-up comedians, are brilliant at doing. They open loops in the story that make the reader want to hang on to their every word.

Blatant examples might be something like, "Jack didn't know what the treasure map told him but he knew it was significant." The reader wants to read on to find out what it is that Jack is about to find out.

Note though that for modern day readers who have read and seen this sort of thing many times, you need to be more subtle than this.

If you read through this book again, you will see it is littered with loops opened earlier in the book, only to be closed later.

The best loop of all to open is the one that subtly implies there's a sequel on the way.

Writing in this manner has a triple benefit. Firstly, you are entranced while you are writing and words just flow. Secondly, your reader is entranced while reading and can't put the book down. Finally, you effortlessly enter that mode where time expands and you get more done.

Like all the tips and techniques in this book, it needs preparation and practice (which is me opening a loop up suggesting you should do the next exercise). The practice is self-fulfilling and you can get better and better at it through the process of writing your first book.

When you come to write your second and third books (more loop opening), you may consciously structure them around nested loop architecture. This is something I cover on my workshops and will be one of the subjects of one of my next books (another big loop opened).

Note, I normally refrain from such blatant pluggery and merely include it here to demonstrate the technique. I read a book recently by a very intelligent chap who must have mentioned at least four or five times in the book that what I really needed to know was in his next book, not in the one that I was reading. This had an effect all right - I didn't buy it.

I hope this example, which I included for explanatory purposes only, doesn't have that effect on you.

Exercise 14: Writing In Trance

To augment this exercise you can listen to the 'Future Entanglement' MP3 Visualisation. Details at the back of the book.

To enter this mode it is vital that you are working without interruptions so plan your writing time, switch off your phones and don't be tempted to answer emails. This is where telling people about your plan to write and your availability helps.

It's also useful if you can meditate before your writing session without feeling rushed. If you get an insight during meditation, don't be tempted to finish and start writing. There may be more to come and you will remember it. If you can't meditate, even a short 10 minute walk is good preparation.

A good connection with your vestigial minds and the super-consciousness are essential so it's worth going over the exercises in chapters 7 to 10.

You need to be focused about what you want to achieve in the next writing session. This is not so much about the words themselves, they will come naturally, but the outcome of the session. This could be that you have another chapter finished or, in this case, that I describe this exercise in a simple manner.

Be mindful also to be writing from a reader-centric perspective as discussed in the last chapter. This encourages disassociation from the task and the suppression of ego.

Set yourself a target which should be small, manageable and meaningful. When you achieve it, take a break and give yourself a reward which could be a cup of tea or a snack.

There is one more technique you can take advantage of when writing in this manner, if you accept that the superconsciousness exists outside our normal space-time and that everyone past, present and future is tapped into it.

The *'you in the future'* and your *'reader in the future'* can access the words you are about to write. If this is so, then it is possible to tap into these words and channel them through the *'you in the present'*.

Now I know this sounds like a plot line from *Back to the Future*, or that it belongs in an episode of *Doctor Who*, but it seems to work. For example, my first book was written before the micro-blogging site Twitter was invented. It turns out that it is a perfect format for a book to be micro-blogged. Was that luck or prescience? It doesn't matter if this all works.

The following diagram shows how such a mechanism might operate.

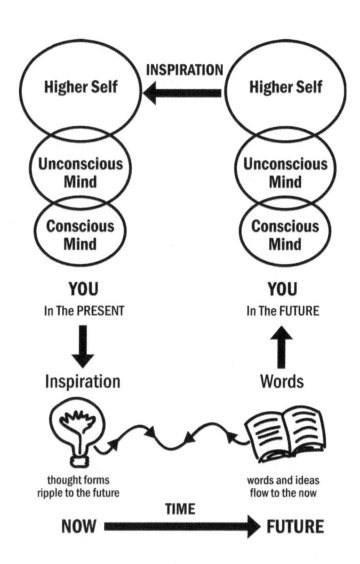

With this in mind, listen to *Future Entanglement* in the MP3 Visualisation Pack which helps set up these connections between you now and in the future.

I am off to make that celebratory cup of tea... enjoy.

CHAPTER 15

Being An Author

"I always start a novel by starting the first and last pages which seem to survive intact through all the following drafts."

Jerry Kosinki, author of *Being There*

Being an author is a state of mind. As you have seen, how you sleep, how you eat and even how you breathe affects how you will write.

It extends further than this.

Once your book is finished and published, however, you can experience a different type of block – and that's author's block.

You may have successfully suppressed your initial fear of failure or ridicule to write a book. A new fear can now overtake you - the fear of success.

You can tell if this is something you are prone to if you find yourself being shy of telling people about your book – or if you find yourself self-sabotaging your success.

Even with a large publishing contract, the best person to sell and promote a book is the author.

If readers like your book, they will become as interested in you as they are in your book.

They will be keen to know about your influences and about what else you are writing, or have written. They may look at your Internet site or your blog and see if you are making any appearances locally.

Being an author requires you to adopt a new state of mind and state of being. This doesn't mean you have to grow, nurture and develop an ego, but that you should be respectful of what you have written and its impact on others.

You will find yourself being presented with new ideas of what to write next. You may be out walking or meditating and a light bulb moment will hit you - showing you the whole of your next book.

Being an author is both a joy and a responsibility. For example, my initial aim for this book is to be a resource for people starting their literary careers. I now realise it is equally useful for authors on their second or third work as it contains insights and exercises to help the creative juices flow. Accordingly, I will be taking broadcasting these messages not just through book sales but in blogs, podcast interviews and workshops.

I could write more and more on this subject but now feel it's appropriate to stop, just in case I encounter the block of never finishing.

I am also comfortable to stop now as I know that after publication of this book, I will be even better able to continue to expand and extrapolate on these themes in books yet to come.

I feel doubly comfortable to stop in the knowledge that this book should purposely short as a long discourse is not recommended reading for anyone suffering from a block.

Thanks for reading and good luck in spreading your words.

Exercise 15: Putting It All Together

To augment this exercise you can listen to the 'Embedding Mind Maps in Your Cellular Neurology' MP3 Visualisation. Details at the back of the book.

Whether you are starting to write your book or you have written one already and are starting the next, there are several steps you can take that will help you on your path. They aren't mandatory and the last thing you should do is give yourself a hard time if you don't manage to accomplish them all.

For example, let's say you get up and plan your morning meditation but the urge to write is strong. So – just write.

- Meditate daily or, if you can't manage it, at least before each writing session – a walk counts as a meditation here.
- Watch what you eat.
- Be mindful of how you breathe.
- Keep a dream diary.
- Notice coincidences.
- Go for walk/cross crawl if stuck.

- Always keep a notepad or a voice recorder handy (most mobile phones can do both nowadays).
- Mind Map chapter structures as opposed to writing them in bullet form.
- *Have fun!*

For each chapter, list:

- Ideas and plot lines.
- Concepts you want to impart.
- Reader state at start.
- Reader state at the end.

Set time aside for writing:

- One chapter or blog each one or two hours.
- Establish the number of days to first draft.
- Establish how many elapsed weeks to first draft.
- Mind Map your goals and milestones.

Treat yourself regularly when you complete each chapter and reach each milestone.

Finally take your Mind Maps and stick them on your walls and have fun again with the MP3 visualisation *Embedding Mind Maps in Your Cellular Neurology.*

Postamble: Voiding Karma

"It only has to be true enough."

Bill Liao, www.neo.org

I have introduced you to some concepts you may not have associated with creative writing. We've looked at models for a collective mind and the idea of using our vestigial minds.

None of these have actually to be true to be of use. If just thinking about them produces a positive benefit and results in you finishing your book, then they are true enough.

As such, I make no claim for their veracity; they are here as I've found they've been incredibly useful with writers I have worked with.

This next concept definitely falls into the "it's true enough" category as it's something that is hard to prove one way or another.

Also it is not my aim to challenge anybody's belief set.

The concept of reincarnation is something that is part of most world religions and it was even an integral part of Christianity a millennia or so ago. After all, it's an attractive concept to think that we come back time and time again, evolving and improving as we go along.

Incidentally, if we think that this is even a remote possibility, it would make sense for us to look after the planet now in case we have to come back to it later.

Whether we do come back or not, our physical DNA is carried forward generation after generation. When you become a published author, your *intellectual DNA* also becomes immortal.

An important aspect of reincarnation is that of **karma**. Karma is the idea that you have learnings to embrace within each lifetime and are sent challenges to help you do so. Note that I don't subscribe to a moralistic standpoint here – that something that has been used for fear-based methods for control and power by both politicians and religions.

As humans we like to systemise and elaborate and it's said we go to a place called the Akashic Records Office at the end of one life and at the start of another. Here we review a life just gone and form a karmic agreement with a soul group of what we aim to achieve in our next incarnation.

If you are interested in exploring this, you can listen to the 'Journey To The Akashic' MP3 Visualisation. Details at the back of the book.

If we are to evolve and learn, the challenges we face are really helpful. If we are faced with blocks that stop us writing, they can be seen in a positive light.

Rather than being disheartened by a blockage, think of how the block can help you.

Blocks

Perhaps the block itself is something you can write about and thus understand it. You achieve catharsis by overcoming the block and then you pass the insights on to your reader.

If you are writing a book on personal development, or some sort of struggle or turmoil, you will encounter blocks specifically in your subject area.

It's also likely that you set about the challenge of writing a book to face demons of the past so you can evolve.

If you learn to love your blocks, they will take on a whole new character and context and you will see remarkable results. As you successfully overcome one block, others come along. It is as if the universe notices you have taken the decision to move on and is systematically helping you do so.

A good sign that it is a block you need to deal with is when you sense a repeat pattern. If three people recommend a film or a book to you, you take notice. Likewise, if you spot the same block coming up again and again, there could be a reason for it.

If, for instance, you are on your third disastrous relationship or have a job with a bullying boss for the third time, it's time to do something about it. You can write about it for starters.

By far the best way to deal with blocks is to learn to love them. In the above cases, this might be difficult but learning to love the blocks and challenges you face seems to bring remarkable results.

Removing blocks in this way is like taking layers off an onion. As you tackle each one, sometimes deeper and deeper challenges come your way. This process is known as **voiding karma** and it is a great life skill to learn. Try it, and note that the opposite approach is to a-void karma.

Above all, remember it just has to be true enough.

About The Author

Tom Evans studied electronic engineering at university before embarking on a career in the broadcasting and internet industries. He was fascinated by what seemed to be the magic of radio and television and to his parents' chagrin took transistor radios apart as a child to see how they worked. Reassembly was not always successful – there were often some bits left over.

He started writing fiction in his late 40s after a light bulb moment following an encounter with a tarantula in a shower.

He became fascinated by where ideas actually came from out of the blue and how our minds generate creative thoughts, or don't.

His research led him to train as a hypnotherapist, a past life regressor and a Mind Map trainer.

He runs regular workshops on how to *Unleash the Book, Blog and Idea Inside You.* He is an entertaining and enlightening speaker and talks on where ideas come from and how to free yourself from creative blocks.

He is a student of the esoteric and exoteric and many colleagues and clients have called him a modern seer, shaman and alchemist. Tom sagely avoids such labels. Nevertheless, his clients report that he seems to be able to help them turn their words into literary gold.

He lives in Surrey in the UK and is lucky to have access to the best resource ever for a blocked writer, two dogs who need walking daily. This book could not have been written without their help.

Wellington & Reuben

Recommended Reading

Time Management for Dummies, Clare Evans - John Wiley & Sons, 2008

The Artist's Way, Julia Cameron - Pan Books, 1995

Science and the Akashic Field, Ervin Lazlo - Inner Traditions, 2007

The Holographic Universe, Michael Talbot - Harper Collins, 1996

How to Mind Map, Tony Buzan - Thorsons, 2002

The Field, Lynne McTaggart - Harper Collins, 2003

Sixth Sense, Dr Laurie Nadel - Asja Press, 1990

Don't Think Like a Human, Lee Carroll - The Kryon Writings, 1994

The Self Aware Universe, Amit Goswami - Tarcher Putnam, 1995

The Phenomenon of Man, Teilhard de Chardin - Perennial, 2002

How to Know the Higher Worlds, Rudolph Steiner - Anthroposophic Press, 1994

Making Time, Stephen Taylor - Icon Books, 2007

Tom Evans

Glossary

Akashic Field is the source of all manifestation and interconnectedness, flowing out and in via the zero-point field with the cosmic mind and universal consciousness. It is the field that unifies all things.

Alpha Chakra is a point an inch or so above the crown of your head which is thought to be the place where your brain-mind connects with the superconsciousness.

Alpha State is where meditation starts and you begin to access the wealth of creativity that lies just below our conscious awareness. It is the gateway that leads into deeper states of consciousness. When you are truly relaxed, your brain activity slows from the rapid patterns of waking beta into the more gentle waves of alpha. Fresh creative energy begins to flow, fears vanish and you experience a liberating sense of peace and well-being.

Benzene Ring is the doughnut-like shape of organic chemical compound with the molecular formula C_6H_6. Benzene is a colourless and highly flammable liquid with a sweet smell.

Brahman is said by the sage-seers of the Upanishads to be the Absolute Reality or universal substrate. It is said to be eternal, omnipotent, omniscient, omnipresent, and ultimately indescribable in human language.

Brain Plasticity is the changing of neurons, the organisation of their networks, and their function resulting from new experiences. It is also referred to as neuroplasticity, cortical plasticity or cortical re-mapping. Recent research though indicates that it is the glial cells (the 90 percent of the brain whose function is not fully understood) not the neurons that are at the root of such changes.

Cerebrospinal Fluid is a clear bodily fluid that occupies the space around and inside the brain. Essentially, the brain *floats* in it. It acts as a cushion or buffer for the cortex, providing mechanical and immunological protection to the brain inside the skull.

Chakras are said to be whorls of energy permeating, from points on the physical body. Some believe the chakras interact with the body's ductless endocrine glands and lymphatic system by feeding in good bio-energies and disposing of unwanted bio-energies.

Claircogniscence is the ability to possess intrinsic knowledge of something or someone where the information was not gleaned in a conventional manner.

Conscious Mind refers to our self awareness, wakefulness and the ability to think. It is thought it can process 7 +/- 2 *things* per second.

Corpus Callosum is a structure of mammalian brains that connects the left and right cerebral hemispheres. It facilitates communication between the two hemispheres.

Cosmic Consciousness is the concept that the universe exists as an interconnected network of consciousness, with each conscious being linked to every other to form a collective consciousness which spans the cosmos.

Essential Fatty Acids (EFAs) are fatty acids that cannot be constructed within an organism from other components by any known chemical pathways, and therefore must be obtained from the diet.

Ethereal and Astral Planes are planes that are thought to exist above, around an inside our physical plane. You must travel through the etheric plane to reach astral and it is reported this is done in dreams and in meditation. They have an equivalence to the Akashic Fields and superconsciousness.

Gestalts are patterns that are established in the brain-mind from individual thoughts and memories that lead to certain behaviours.

Glycemic Index refers to the rate at which sugar from a particular food enters the cells of the body. As such, it is a measure of the effects of carbohydrates on blood sugar levels.

Grand Mal Seizure is where there is excessive or synchronous neuronal activity in the brain. It can manifest as an alteration in mental state, convulsions and even psychic symptoms such as déjà vu.

Heart Chakra is the central chakra of your personality energy field; it is here you begin integrating your spiritual awareness & physical experience. The heart chakra is associated with acceptance and love for others unconditionally. It accepts both positive and negative qualities. Characteristics of a blocked heart chakra include fear of rejection, feeling unworthy of love or loving too much.

Hemispheric Lateralisation of brain function is a term coined by Professor Sperry, and others, to describe how different motor and cognitive functions seem to reside in different sides of the brain both in the cortex and lower brain regions.

Higher Self is thought to be the part of our psyche that exists outside our physical bodies but that connects us to the superconsciousness and higher planes.

Hypnagogic State is the wonderful state just between being awake and falling asleep. It occurs in day dreaming too.

Hypnopompic State is the state between sleeping and waking which is the best place to remain in order to recall your dreams.

Karma is a Sanskrit word that means action. Karma has commonly been considered a punishment for past bad actions, but karma is neither judge nor jury. Rather, it is simply the universal law of cause and effect that says every thought, word and act carries energy into the world and affects our present reality. Karma can also refer to the work we have ahead of us, which includes lessons from both our past and present lives.

Lucid Dreams are extremely real and vivid dreams in which you are aware you are dreaming. You can actively participate in and often manipulate the imaginary experiences in the dream environment.

Mind Mapping is a diagramming method where words, ideas and tasks are arranged around a central key word or image. Mind Maps are used to generate, visualise, structure, and classify ideas and as aids in study, organisation, problem solving, decision making, and, of course, writing.

Morphic Field is a concept coined primarily by Rupert Sheldrake where our life force and mental energy forms a pattern in the collective consciousness which forms a resonance with similarly shaped patterns. It explains how salamanders might re-grow tails and how your dog might know you are coming home.

Neo-Consciousness refers to new states of consciousness which are entered into via the meditative state. It is also thought that we are entering a new phase of cogniscence.

Neurotransmitters are chemicals which relay, amplify and modulate signals between a neuron and another cell across the synaptic gaps.

Noosphere was coined by Teilhard de Chardin, and others, to describe the collective consciousness of human-beings. Others, such as James Lovelock, extended the idea to include all life forms and the Earth, or Gaia, itself.

Out of Body Experiences (OBEs) describe dream-like or even near-death states where you literally feel like you are out of your body. Crash victims or patients undergoing surgery have reported events that they could not have recalled or details of areas in the operating room they simply could not have seen even if they were awake.

Pilates is a discipline which focuses on the core postural muscles which help keep the body balanced and which are essential to providing support for the spine. In particular, Pilates exercises teach awareness of breath and alignment of the spine, and aim to strengthen the deep internal muscles.

Pineal Gland is a small endocrine gland in the vertebrate brain. It produces melatonin, a hormone that affects the modulation of our waking and sleep patterns. It is shaped like a tiny pine cone (hence its name), and is located near to the centre of the brain, between the two hemispheres. It is thought to be the primary connection point for our Higher Self and is also known as the psychic gland and third eye.

Qi Gong is a Chinese meditative practice which uses slow graceful movements and controlled breathing techniques to promote the circulation of Qi, or life force, within the human body.

Quantum Collapse of Thought refers to our inability to have a thought and think about it at the same time. It is also not possible to measure the position and momentum of sub-atomic particles, which is known as Heisenberg's Uncertainty Principle. For this reason, by equivalence, it is thought that thoughts also exhibit quantum behaviour.

Satori is a Japanese Zen Buddhist term for enlightenment. The word literally means understanding and describes a flash of sudden awareness, or individual enlightenment which is also known in the West as a light bulb moment.

Seasonal Affective Disorder (SAD) is a mood disorder where people who have normal mental health throughout most of the year experience depressive symptoms in the winter and, less frequently, in the summer, spring or autumn.

Serotonin functions as a neurotransmitter in nerve systems of simple as well as complex animals and is known to play an important role in the modulation of mood, anger and aggression.

Solar Plexus Chakra is the power centre of your body and mediates the energies relating to your willpower, purpose and creativity. If this chakra is functioning you feel a warm glow like the fire this chakra represents. If the solar plexus chakra is blocked, then you likely feel easily depressed and rejected and possibly wanting to blame others for your insecurity feelings.

Superconsciousness is the concept that the universe exists as an interconnected network of consciousness, with each conscious being linked to every other to form a collective consciousness which spans the cosmos. The idea bears similarity to Carl Jung's Collective Unconscious, Teilhard de Chardin's concept of the Noosphere, James Lovelock's Gaia Theory and to Satori in Zen.

Synaesthetes are people who have a perceptual experience from one sense that gives rise to an experience in different sensory modality. An example might be a smell that gives the sense of the colour green or hearing a sound in response to a flickering light.

Tai Chi has roots as a martial art and focuses the mind solely on the movements of what is known as *"The Form"* which helps to bring about a state of mental calm and clarity.

Taoism is a philosophy rather than a religion that have influenced East Asia for over two millennia. The word Tao means 'path' or 'way' and, if you are on it, life becomes effortless. The Taoists advocate never using more force or energy than you absolutely have to and, essentially, to go with the flow.

Throat Chakra is located at your larynx. It represents the point in your awareness where all your experiences are welcomed without judgment. With an open throat chakra you are comfortable in expressing yourself to others, whatever it is that may need to be said. Blockages manifest themselves as a lack self-expression or even writer's block.

Theta State is where brain activity slows, in meditation, almost to the point of sleep. Theta brings forward heightened receptivity, flashes of dream-like imagery, inspiration, and, sometimes, long-forgotten memories. It can also give you a sensation of floating or even initiate an OBE. Theta is one of the more elusive and extraordinary realms you can explore. It is a natural state which you experience at least twice a day at the hypnagogic and hypnopompic points.

Third Eye is thought to be located in the pineal gland and is also a chakra point. An engorged third eye is thought to be the basis for the myth of the Cyclops. With practice, you can actually see the whirling vortex of your third eye chakra.

Tomography is the process of imaging living tissue by sections or slices, often using devices such as PET, CAT and MRI scanners.

Tryptophan is an essential amino acid. This means that it cannot be synthesised by us and therefore must be part of our diet. It is thought to increase the brain's production of serotonin and subsequently to elevate our mood.

Tyrosine is another amino acid that increases neurotransmitter activity. It is often used to treat withdrawal symptoms.

Vestigial Minds refers to the concept that our mind is not just co-located in our brains but at all our chakras points and, indeed, in every cell of our body. The vestigial nature is simply that our education and culture has tended to focus on the predominant mind centre being the brain leading to atrophy in the use of the other minds.

Vestigial Organs are organs that once had a function and are no longer needed but still exist as a remnant in our bodies.

Voiding Karma is the process of realising your karmic mission and purpose and consolidating your learnings so that you can evolve further.

Whole-Brain-Thinking is using both right and left hemispheres of your brain in a way that 1+1 > 2.

Whole-Mind-Not-Thinking is where your conscious mind becomes inextricably linked to your unconscious and vestigial minds such that you are not aware of conscious thought but totally *in the zone*, yet cogniscent and amazingly creative and productive.

Yin and Yang represents the concept where everything is comprised of two forces or principles. One being negative, dark, passive, cold, wet, and feminine (Yin) and the other positive, bright, active, dry, hot and masculine (Yang). The interactions and balance of these forces in people and nature influence their behaviour and fate. The breath is also the mediator of these forces.

Contact Tom

For more information about Tom, his workshops and his one-to-one mentoring services for authors, visit his blog site: **www.thebookwright.com**

Tom can be contacted directly at **tom@thebookwright.com**

You can also follow Tom's musings, memes and observations on Twitter at **www.twitter.com/thebookwright**

Feedback and reviews are gratefully received.

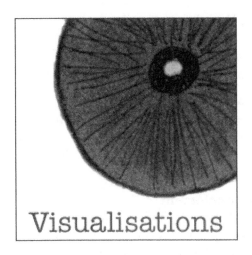

Visualisations

The exercises in this book can be augmented by listening to accompanying MP3 visualisations.

These visualisations use brain entrainment background audio to take the brain into alpha and theta states.

Embedding Mind Maps in your Neurology
This allows you to take any Mind Map, or image, and embeds it into your cellular neurology such that you remember it intrinsically. You will also start to notice coincidences and associations related to the Mind Map.

Quantum Collapse of Thought
This is ideal for those who have never experienced the meditative state and have trouble quietening the mind. Once you have listened to this meditation several times you will be able to remember it and perform it by yourself.

Becoming Fear-less

This visualisation takes you on a journey to becoming a successful published author and tackles the common fears we all experience along the way.

Re-minding Yourself

Use this visualisation to reconnect with your gut and heart minds. Once your third eye is clear for pure thought, you can then connect effortlessly to the superconsciousness.

Future Entanglement

This visualisation uses timeline techniques to entangle the *you in the present* with a version of *you in the future*. Once connected, you will be drawn down a path to success.

Journey to the Akashic Records

Journey back in time to the point between lives where we discuss and agree our karmic purpose. You will be connected with the *real you* and emerge with a new sense of purpose for why you are here and what you are writing.

You can buy and download these visualisations from
www.thebookwright.com/visualisations

Your 30 Day Free Trial of The Publishing Academy

Once you've overcome writer's block for good, you may want to improve your success in another area of your writing endeavours.

The Publishing Academy was created to provide authors with help, support and winning techniques at every stage of the publishing process – from ideas to making a fulltime income as an author.

So, for details of a very special offer where you'll also get a free 30-day-pass to the exclusive Publishing Academy members-only area, worth £15.00, go to:

http://www.publishingacademy.com/105-7-1-3.html

We look forward to seeing you there and sharing more with you in the future. So keep on visiting and learning from Tom and the other experts when you become part of *www.publishingacademy.com*.

The Wealthy Author

The Fast Profit Method For Writing, Publishing & Selling Your Non-Fiction Book

JOE GREGORY
DEBBIE JENKINS

www.publishingacademy.com

PUBLISHING ACADEMY
OFFICIAL GUIDEBOOK

THE
Amazon
Bestseller
PLAN

HOW TO MAKE YOUR BOOK
AN AMAZON BESTSELLER
IN 24 HOURS OR LESS

DEBBIE JENKINS
JOE GREGORY

www.publishingacademy.com

Get Your
Book
Published

HOW TO DEVISE, WRITE & SELL YOUR NON-FICTION BOOK TO PUBLISHERS

SUZAN ST MAUR

www.publishingacademy.com

Made in the USA
Middletown, DE
16 June 2020